JB
NIX
ON

Hargrove, Jim

Richard M. Nixon,
the thirty-seventh
president

JB
NIX
ON

Hargrove, Jim

Richard M. Nixon,
the thirty-seventh
president

DATE

BORROWER'S NAME

THE BAKER & TAYLOR CO.

Richard M. Nixon

The Thirty-seventh President

by Jim Hargrove

CHILDRENS PRESS™

CHICAGO

PICTURE ACKNOWLEDGMENTS

United Press International Photo—Frontispiece, pages 6, 73,
74 (2 photos), 75 (2 photos), 76 (2 photos), 77 (2 photos), 78 (2 photos),
79 (2 photos)
Cover illustration by David J. Catrow III

Library of Congress Cataloging in Publication Data

Hargrove, Jim
  Richard M. Nixon, the thirty-seventh president.

  Includes index.
  Summary: A survey of the life of Richard Nixon,
including his youth in California, rise in politics, election
as president, and resignation after Watergate.
  1. Nixon, Richard M. (Richard Milhous), 1913-
Juvenile literature. 2. United States—Politics and
government—1969-1974—Juvenile literature. 3. Presidents—
United States—Biography—Juvenile literature.
[1. Nixon, Richard M. (Richard Milhous), 1913-
2. Presidents. 3. United States—Politics and government—
1969-1974] I. Title.
E856.H37   1985   973.924′092′4 [92]   84-27416
ISBN 0-516-03212-7

1 2 3 4 5 6 7 8 9 10 R 94 93 92 91 90 89 88 87 86 85

Table of Contents

Chapter 1

GROWING UP IN CALIFORNIA

For centuries, America has been known as the land of opportunity. For the Europeans who were its earliest white settlers, America offered an escape from unchanging patterns of life in the Old Country. Before America was settled, Europeans who were born to poor families were almost certain to remain poor throughout their lives. People who were born to special wealthy families, often called the *nobility*, might become kings or queens or have other titles of power. Poor farmers, tradesmen, and merchants had little chance to join the governing class.

But in America all that changed. Andrew Jackson, the seventh president of the United States, rose to the highest office in the newly settled land after being born—and soon orphaned—in the backwoods of the Carolinas. Abraham Lincoln became America's sixteenth president even though he was born to poor farmers in a tiny log cabin.

Richard Nixon, who would become the thirty-seventh president, was not raised in a log cabin. Instead, he was born in a small frame house, the log cabin of the twentieth century, which had been built by his father, Frank Nixon. Frank Nixon chose to build his modest house in the small town of Yorba Linda, not far from Los Angeles. For many, California seemed like one of the last remnants of the American frontier.

The Nixon family had been part of America's growth from the British settlements of the 1700s to an important world power in the twentieth century. Frank Nixon's great-grandfather, George Nixon, had fought in the revolutionary war. His grandfather, also named George, had fought at Gettysburg, an important battle in the Civil War.

In 1886, when Frank was seven years old, his mother died. His father, who worked as a farmer, a teacher, and a mail carrier, had not been able to support his family. The family of five brothers and one sister was broken up and the children were forced to live with other relatives, mostly in Ohio.

During the early 1900s, Frank worked as a streetcar conductor in the city of Columbus, Ohio. But the cold winters in Columbus must have made him dream about the warm climate of California. There, he would be away from the freezing streetcar that was never properly heated during the cold Ohio winters. And, he thought, perhaps he could even buy some land in California and begin farming vegetables or growing fruit. He packed what he needed and boarded a train for Los Angeles in 1907.

Frank Nixon wasn't the only American who dreamed about southern California. For many generations of Americans, southern California has been a land of dreams. By the mid-1800s, the discovery of gold in the hills east of the Pacific coastline brought thousands of prospectors to California, adding more settlers to the American pioneers and Spanish missionaries who had arrived earlier. Even when the gold became scarce, the warm, sunny climate and the rich farmlands in the valleys of southern California made many a tired old prospector just want to stay for a while.

By the time Frank Nixon arrived in Los Angeles the gold was largely gone. And unlike the pioneers who had arrived nearly a century before him, he could not receive the rich farmland free. Although he dreamed of being a citrus fruit farmer, Frank had to find work once again as a streetcar operator. A trolley car company called the Los Angeles Street Railway had built tracks joining Los Angeles with the smaller town of Whittier to the east. Frank got a job with the company the same year. At a party for motormen the following year, he met a young woman named Hannah Milhous.

For many generations the Milhous family had been Quakers, members of the Society of Friends church. Although its numbers were never that large, the Quaker church has had an important influence in American history. Opposed to war, alcohol, human injustice, even music and dancing, the stern system of Quaker beliefs helped develop hard work and religious devotion in its followers.

Thomas Milhous, the first American member of the family and a devout Quaker, came to Pennsylvania from Ireland in 1729. Several generations of Milhouses gradually moved west, to Ohio in 1805, Indiana in 1854, and, finally California in 1897. Hannah's father, Franklin, was married twice. His first wife died giving birth to their second child. His second wife, Almira, had six girls and one boy. Hannah was born on March 7, 1885, in Butlerville, Indiana. When Franklin and Almira moved their family of nine children, including Hannah, to Whittier in 1897, they chose the town that would mark the end of the line for eastbound cars on Frank Nixon's trolley run ten years later.

Frank Nixon fell in love with Hannah Milhous from almost the first moment he met her. In order to gain acceptance from Hannah's family, Frank decided to become a Quaker. They were married on June 25, 1908, in Whittier. Their first child, Harold, was born on June 1, 1909. With the help of the Milhous family, Frank and Hannah bought a citrus grove in the nearby town of Yorba Linda in 1911.

In the same year that the young couple purchased their fruit farm, the first motion picture studio opened in a new section of Los Angeles called Beverly Hills. The movie industry would grow and grow, before long becoming the most important and well-known business in and around Los Angeles. Thousands of people would find jobs with the companies that produced movies. A few would become rich and famous. More than anything else, the motion picture business would establish southern California's reputation as the land of dreams.

But Frank and Hannah's dream had nothing to do with the movies. They hoped to make their fortune growing and selling citrus fruit in the grove at Yorba Linda. They worked hard to make their dream come true.

The citrus grove the Nixons bought would eventually fail. But even though it never brought much money to the young family, Frank managed to build a house nearby. He was a good carpenter, and must have had a number of other skills needed for such a project. The Nixons' second boy, Richard, was born on January 9, 1913, in the house that Frank built.

On the chilly January night that the thirty-seventh president of the United States was born, the small frame house in Yorba Linda was warm and comfortable. But it was not always that way. Built for the tropical climate of southern California, the house was often chilly in winter.

With two babies, the Nixon family believed it had good reason to worry about wintry temperatures. At the time of Richard Nixon's birth, a disease called tuberculosis killed more people than any other. It was thought, incorrectly, that the sickness tended to occur in certain families when the weather was cold and damp. A number of children in the Milhous family had died from the dreaded disease. The Nixon family, too, had known its dangers.

The full name Frank and Hannah gave to their second son

was Richard Milhous Nixon. Richard was the name of three famous English kings of the past. Milhous, of course, was Hannah's maiden name. Unlike his older brother, Harold, Richard was not known as a quiet baby. His mother remembered for many years how often and how loudly Richard would cry.

In a land where iron horses and horseless carriages were slowly replacing the fabled horse of the American West, Richard Nixon spent his entire youth. But several of his earliest and most frightening experiences were centered around the gradually vanishing workhorse.

When Richard was two years old, his father got a job with the Anaheim Union Water Company digging ditches to control rainwater. For some reason, the father took his young son with him to work one day. There Richard saw a team of huge horses the company used to help dig the ditches. He began crawling right behind some of the horses that were straining backward to pull a heavy load. In seconds, he could have been trampled by the heavy workhorses. Fortunately, a worker noticed the dangerous situation and pulled Richard away just in time.

Less than a year later, Richard's life was again threatened in an accident involving a horse. Later, when he was an adult, Nixon remarked that this accident was his earliest childhood memory. In a book about his life, he wrote: "I was three years old, and my mother was driving us in a horse-drawn buggy, holding my baby brother Don on her lap while a neighbor girl held me. The horse turned the corner leading to our house at high speed, and I tumbled onto the ground. I must have been in shock, but I managed to get up and run after the buggy while my mother tried to make the horse stop."

Before he could get up, the heavy wheel of the wagon grazed his head, leaving a deep cut. Richard had to be rushed by automobile to a doctor twenty-five miles away, who closed the wound with stitches. A scar remained, but it was eventually covered by his dark blond hair.

Most Quaker households operated under strict rules of behavior, and the Nixon family was no different. Hannah seldom raised her voice, even when disciplining her children, but Frank sometimes had a bad temper when dealing with his kids. Once, when Richard and his brothers Harold and Francis were still quite young, they went swimming in a water ditch near their home. Swimming in the deep ditch was dangerous, and Frank had often told his children not to play there. When he saw his three children swimming in the forbidden ditch, he became very angry.

Frank ran to the ditch and ordered the young boys to get out. "You come out of that water right now!" he yelled. But as the children started scrambling out, Frank's temper got the better of him. "Do you like water?" he shouted at the frightened children. "Have some more of it!" And with those words he threw the brothers one by one back into the ditch. He might have thrown them in again, but a neighbor, fearing for the children's lives, convinced him to stop.

Although he could become quite angry, Frank usually managed to keep his temper under control. But despite his father's temper, Richard feared his mother's disapproval even more. "We dreaded far more than my father's hand, her tongue," he once remarked. Hannah never yelled and seldom lost her temper. But her calm voice and firm beliefs could make her judgments, at times, all the more fearsome.

"Everyone who ever knew my mother was impressed by what a remarkable woman she was," Nixon wrote years later. "When she met and married my father, she had completed her second year of college. They had five sons and, with the exception of one named for my father, she named us after the early kings of England: Harold, born in 1909; Richard, born in 1913; Francis Donald, born in 1914; Arthur, born in 1918; and Edward, born in 1930."

Until 1929, Hannah's quiet, reserved behavior kept a steadying influence on the Nixon household. Prayer, usually silent, was held each morning before breakfast. On Sundays, there were three or four church meetings to attend. Throughout the week, there were plenty of chores to do around the house and in the citrus grove, which, in later life, Richard also called an orange ranch or lemon grove.

Today, citrus farmers allow grass and weeds to grow

around the trunks of their fruit trees. These plants help hold moisture from rainwater and keep the soil from running off. But in the early 1920s some growers, including the Nixons, pulled up all the weeds around the trees. The job of pulling up weeds took many hours every week. With this chore and many others, Richard had little time for play between the end of school and bedtime.

There was some room in his busy schedule, though, to work on a skill that would bring him much enjoyment throughout his life. Since the earliest grades of elementary school, he had taken piano lessons from his uncle, Griffith Milhous. Richard studied hard and practiced seriously. But he also seemed to enjoy just fooling around with the keys, slowly learning to pick out the tunes of the day. When he was a few years older, his parents arranged for him to live for six months with his Aunt Jane. She was a piano teacher, schooled at the Metropolitan School of Music in Indianapolis, who had moved with her family to Lindsay, California.

Everyone who knew Richard as a young boy remembers that he was a serious student at school. A cousin, Jessamyn West, remembered that Richard could argue about the strong and weak points of people running for political offices, especially president of the United States, as early as the second grade, when Warren G. Harding was running for president. Thinking about what he wanted to do when he grew up, Richard does not seem to have dreamed about quite so high an office. He has written that among his earliest memories was the dream to become a railroad engineer.

In 1922, Frank and Hannah's dream of a profitable citrus farm in Yorba Linda had finally withered away. In his memoirs, Nixon described what happened next:

"In 1922 my father sold our house and lemon [citrus] grove in Yorba Linda, and moved to Whittier. He did roustabout work in the oil fields, but although it paid well, the physical labor offered no challenge to a man of his ambition, intelligence, and lively imagination. Early on, my father could see that even though there were still very few automobiles and only one paved road in the area, the horseless carriage was an idea whose time was about to come. He borrowed $5,000 to buy some land on the main road connecting the growing towns of Whittier and La Habra. He cleared the lot, put in a tank and a pump, and opened the first service station in the eight-mile stretch between the two towns."

Soon, Frank decided to sell groceries and some of Hannah's baked goods to the motorists who pulled into the station. The service station and store gave the Nixon family a fairly steady income. Each member, including Richard, worked behind the counter and had many other chores.

At East Whittier Elementary School, Richard was already showing a talent for debates in 1925. His class was debating the topic, "It is better to own your own home than to rent." Along with his parents, Richard believed that it was better to own a home than to rent one. But he showed what a good speaker he was by arguing just the opposite during the debate. He actually convinced many of his classmates that it was better to rent than to own.

Despite the early success of the service station, the move to Whittier did not bring happy years to the Nixon family. Not long after they moved to Whittier, Richard's brothers Arthur and Harold began to show signs of a serious disease, the one the Milhous family especially dreaded: tuberculosis. This may have been the real reason for sending Richard away to study piano with his aunt—to protect him from catching the disease. For Arthur, the end came relatively quickly. He died in 1925.

Harold's battle with tuberculosis lasted much longer. For more than ten years, Frank and Hannah would struggle to keep Harold alive. First, Harold was sent to an expensive private hospital. Then, believing that the dry climate would help his condition, Frank and Hannah rented a cottage for him in California's Antelope Valley. But by 1929, it was clear that Harold's condition was not improving.

It was decided that Hannah would move with Harold to Prescott, Arizona. The dry desert air there was thought to be a cure for tuberculosis. For the better part of three years, Hannah and Harold lived in Arizona, a fourteen-hour drive from the Nixon home in Whittier. During Christmas and spring vacations, Frank, Richard, and Richard's brother

Don would make the long drive to Prescott to be with Hannah and Harold. While in Arizona, Richard worked at all kinds of odd jobs, including a frontier rodeo, to help the family make ends meet.

Harold's worsening health made family life difficult throughout most of Richard's high school and college years. Although he found time to join a number of organizations while he was attending Whittier High School, life at home was not easy. Before she had moved to Arizona, Hannah had done much of the work at the store. Without her, it became difficult for Frank, Richard, and Don to run the store and service station efficiently.

Despite the difficult conditions at home, Richard managed to develop a good reputation for studies while he was in high school. Although he lost his first election, for student-body president during his junior year, the teachers appointed him student-body manager. As manager, he had interesting jobs selling football tickets and persuading local businesses to buy advertisements in the school yearbook. He won contests in speech two years in a row, and in his senior year won the Harvard Club of California's award for outstanding all-round student.

In his junior year, Richard had the lead male role in the school play. By his own admission, Richard's acting debut was not much of a success, but he did perform with a student named Ola-Florence Welch, who would be his girl friend for several years. Like playing the piano, acting on the stage was a source of fun for him for a number of years. He must have enjoyed his roles very much. Time away from his difficult home life probably was hard to come by. Although he eventually stopped seeing Ola-Florence Welch, it would be through acting, some years later, that Richard would meet the young woman who became his wife.

While he was still in high school, Richard dreamed of attending one of the famous colleges in the East, a great university such as Harvard or Yale. After all, his high-school grades were good, and he was graduated third in his class. But by 1930, his senior year, it was clear that his dream would not come true. Even with a scholarship, the Nixons could not afford to send Richard to an expensive school. America's Great Depression had just begun. Nobody, it seemed, was left with any money.

Anxious to continue his studies, Richard decided to become a student at Whittier College, where he could continue learning and still help out at home. In college he continued to do many of the things he had done in high school. Of course, he studied very hard. He acted in many of the plays put on by students and even worked as a stage manager in several musicals. He also joined the football team. He was not large or strong enough to be a star, but there were only eleven men on the freshman team, so he played every game that year. He enjoyed the team spirit, even though in later years he almost always had to cheer his team on from the bench.

Football may not have been his greatest talent, but it was already becoming clear that he could get people to vote for him. Richard was elected president of his junior class.

Life at home took a long-feared turn when Harold lost his struggle of more than a decade with tuberculosis. For years he had been terribly thin and in such bad physical condition that he was exhausted and out of breath just walking to the house.

For more than ten years, Hannah Nixon had devoted much of her life to saving the lives of two of her sons. She had lost in both struggles, and both had taken their toll around the Nixon household. With a new baby, Edward, born in 1930, Frank and Hannah had to sell much of their business in order to make ends meet.

But life at Whittier College was beginning to open new doors for Richard. His excellent grades, fine debating skills, and carefully well-rounded extracurricular activities were admired by Ola-Florence, as well as many of the other students. In May of 1934, Nixon learned the exciting news that he had been offered a scholarship to attend Duke University Law School in North Carolina. When he accepted the prize, he took his first great step on a march to the most important job in the United States.

Chapter 2

YOUNG MR. NIXON

Richard's success as a student at Whittier College was remarkable. He was graduated in 1934 with the second highest grades in his class; always a hard-working scholar, he had served as president of his junior class, a football and basketball player, a debater, and a member of a singing club. His classmates remembered him as the kind of student who always put his studies first.

At Duke University there was an even greater demand for serious study. Richard's scholarship was for $250 a year, which may not seem like very much today. But in the 1930s, during the worst part of the Great Depression, it paid the full tuition at Duke University Law School. It would make it possible for him to become a lawyer.

But there was one serious catch. The university gave out a number of scholarships to first-year students each year. But the number of scholarships would be cut in half for the second year. Only students in the top half of the group would be offered free studies. The law students themselves called the scholarship program "the meat grinder."

Some of his classmates at Duke Law School remembered Richard as someone who would "study himself sick." He

21

really didn't need to worry about his grades. When he was graduated in June of 1937, he ranked third in his class. But well before graduation, there were other concerns for him.

The most important was to find a job to begin after graduating. While attending law school, he worked in the law library and did research for a teacher. But with his schooling nearly complete, it was now time to find a full-time job in the practice of law.

With two of his classmates, he visited a number of large offices in New York City during the Christmas vacation of 1936. Although his friends were able to find jobs, Richard was not. At the time, jobs were very hard to come by. He also applied to the Federal Bureau of Investigation, hoping, probably, to become an FBI agent. After being invited for an interview, it was more than fifteen years before he heard anything further about his application. When he was vice-president of the United States during the 1950s, he asked FBI Director J. Edgar Hoover about his application. Hoover looked into the matter and called back, saying that his application had been approved, but the budget had been cut before the announcement, preventing additional hiring.

As a top graduate of a major law school, young Mr. Nixon knew that, despite the difficult job market, he would be able to find work in many different parts of the country. But it was to Whittier that he decided to return—perhaps the sunny California climate helped make his decision.

As soon as he arrived in Whittier, Richard began studying for the California bar exam, a three-day test on the laws of California that all lawyers in the state were required to pass. He was particularly worried about knowing California laws, which he had not studied at all at Duke. After three weeks of study night and day, he took the test. Then anxiously at his parents' home, he waited and waited days for the results of the test to come by mail. When the official package finally arrived, he had to open it in the bathroom so his mother would not see how nervous he was. But the news was good; he had passed. He could now work as a lawyer in the state of California.

Richard found a job with Whittier's oldest law firm, Wingert and Bewley, where he worked from 1937 until 1941. A year after he started, he was made a partner in the successful company. But the road to becoming a good laywer was not an easy one. In his very first case in court, Richard almost ruined his career.

In that case, Richard was hired by a woman who was trying to collect the money for a loan she had given to a married couple. When a judge ruled that the loan had to be repaid, Nixon decided to sell some land the couple owned to pay off the debt. Then he bought the land himself, for $2,300. Too late, he discovered that several other people were part owners of the land, and that he had no right to sell (or buy) the property.

Few people remembered this early problem until, in 1975, Irving Wallace and his son published *The People's Almanac*, a book that described Richard Nixon's first legal case. A lawyer who would not allow his name to be reported told Mr. Wallace that a judge in that old case had threatened to have Richard disbarred. This meant that Nixon would no longer have been allowed to practice law in the state of California. He might well have had trouble practicing his profession in other states as well.

Fortunately, no action was taken against Richard personally, although his law firm was sued and had to make a payment to Richard's client. But despite his serious mistake, he became a successful lawyer for the firm of Wingert and Bewley. "I enjoyed being a lawyer," he wrote years later in his autobiography, "and after a year the firm became Wingert, Bewley and Nixon. Now for the first time I was no longer Frank and Hannah Nixon's son—I was Mr. Nixon, the new partner in Wingert and Bewley."

Young Mr. Nixon, partly to help bring business to his legal firm, became a member of a number of different clubs and organizations in California. One of them was Whittier's Little Theatre group, where he could continue one of his favorite hobbies—acting on stage. He played an attorney in a drama called *The Night of January 16th* and enjoyed the experience so much that he decided to try out for a role in another play, *The Dark Tower*.

At tryouts for parts in *The Dark Tower*, Nixon met a young high-school teacher named Thelma Catherine Ryan. Everyone called the pretty young redhead "Pat," and from their first meeting Richard knew that he was in love. His first girl friend, Ola-Florence, had married someone else in 1936. Even two years later, it was a painful memory for the young lawyer.

At the Little Theatre, Nixon got a friend to introduce him to Pat. Then he offered to give both a ride home. "On the way I asked Pat if she would like a date with me," he later wrote. "She said, 'I'm very busy.' I said, 'You shouldn't say that, because someday I am going to marry you!' We all laughed because it seemed so unlikely at that time."

Like her future husband, Pat Ryan had had a difficult childhood. Her mother died of cancer when Pat was only thirteen, and before she could enter college her father became seriously ill with a disease called silicosis, probably caused by his work as a miner. She nursed him for two years until his death. After working at several jobs in New York City, Pat returned to California where she went to the University of Southern California. While a college student, she supported herself with a number of different jobs. Pat got some small parts in several Hollywood movies, including *Becky Sharp* and *Small Town Girl*. She was graduated from the University of Southern California in 1937, the same year that Nixon got his law degree from Duke University.

When the two met, Pat had just started a new job teaching business courses at Whittier High School. From that point on, they were together often. Enjoying many of the same activities, Richard and Pat frequently went swimming at Pacific beaches, skiing in the mountains east of Los Angeles, and attended many movies and football games. Richard gave Pat an engagement ring in May of 1940 and they were married on June 21 of the same year.

For a honeymoon, the newlyweds decided to spend several weeks driving through Mexico. To save money, they took a collection of canned foods along in the car. But no sooner had the trip begun than they discovered that their friends had removed all the labels from the cans. For two weeks, practically every meal was a surprise.

For about a year, Richard returned to his work as a lawyer in Whittier, and Pat went back to her classes at the town's high school. In the summer of 1941, the couple took their last vacation for a number of years. Aboard a freight and passenger ship in the Caribbean, they learned the news that the German army under Adolf Hitler had invaded Russia.

In December of 1941, Richard was offered a job with the Office of Price Administration in Washington, D.C. This large government organization was responsible for setting fair prices for a number of different items, especially those in short supply, such as automobile tires and other rubber products. Although the salary was only $3,200 a year, less than the couple was making in California, Pat and Richard decided to move to Washington so that they could learn more about the workings of the federal government. Just before they left for the long drive east, they learned the news that Japanese airplanes had bombed the American naval base at Pearl Harbor in the Hawaiian Islands. The United States was at war!

Hannah Nixon was glad to hear the news that her son would be working at an office in Washington. Many young men and even some young women, she knew, would be joining the armed forces to fight in World War II. Since fighting of any kind, even against a madman such as Adolf Hitler, was against her Quaker beliefs, she hoped that her son would spend the war in a Washington office.

But it was not to be. Although Richard worked at the new job for about eight months, it was not a happy time for him. There were many things about the large government office that he did not like. Many of the people at the Office of Price Administration, he discovered, found ways to make more work for themselves just to make their jobs seem more important. Even worse, some employees seemed to get drunk with power, interested mostly in pushing people around and making small fortunes for themselves.

Despite his Quaker background and the peaceful beliefs of his family, Richard joined the navy in August of 1942. He was sent to an officer training school in Rhode Island where, he later wrote, "I learned to stand straight and keep my shoes shined." After two months, he was sent to a new naval air station in Iowa. Pat moved to Iowa with her husband and got a job as a bank teller. But although life in Iowa was pleasant enough, the young naval officer felt that he should be closer to the fighting. He was just young enough—twenty-nine—to be eligible for duty overseas, and so he applied for the work.

Nixon was ordered to report to San Francisco. From there he would leave for islands in the Pacific Ocean where the battles of World War II were raging. On the way, he stopped in Whittier to say good-bye to his mother and other members of his family. The visit was not a happy one. Although little was said, it was obvious that his family did not approve of his decision to join the war effort.

Although he was never involved in actual battle, Nixon served an important role in the navy. He helped bring supplies to the soldiers who were fighting the Japanese and helped send wounded soldiers home. At least once, his base was bombed by the Japanese and he saw firsthand the terrible results of war. By the time his service was complete, he had earned four medals from the United States government. And although his family would have been shocked, he also learned how to play poker with other sailors, and became an expert player. During the quiet hours of the war, he made a lot of money gambling. He enjoyed playing so much that he once turned down an invitation to have dinner with his commanding officer and the famous airplane pilot Charles Lindbergh. That same night he planned to play in a poker game that had been arranged some weeks earlier.

By July of 1944, Nixon had completed his overseas duty and was ordered to return to the United States. He spent the remaining months of the war working for the navy in many different cities, including San Diego, Washington, Philadelphia, and New York City. In August of 1945, the Nixons joined the huge crowds at Times Square in New York City, celebrating the Japanese surrender and the end of World War II.

Like millions of other Americans who had been involved in one way or another in the war effort, the Nixons now had to decide what to do in peacetime. Richard still had not been released from the navy and Pat was expecting their first child. It was time to think of a career. But before he could give the matter much thought, he received a short letter from Herman Perry, a family friend and important Republican from Whittier. The letter read:

Dear Dick:
I am writing this short note to ask if you would like to be a candidate for Congress on the Republican ticket in 1946.

Jerry Voorhis expects to run—registration is about 50-50. The Republicans are gaining.

Please airmail me your reply if you are interested.

Yours very truly,
H.L. Perry

P.S. Are you a registered voter in California?

Pat and Richard talked about the interesting offer for two days. With Richard's navy pay and considerable poker winnings, and Pat's salary, the couple had managed to save about $10,000 during the war. If Richard decided to run for Congress, he would need much of this money to support himself and Pat, at least until he won the nomination and the Republican party could then help out with finances.

After considering the offer, he called Herman Perry to say that he was interested in running for Congress. Mr. Perry explained that Richard would have to come to California and talk to Republican leaders in Whittier. These leaders would decide which person to back for the Republican nomination. Then, people from Whittier and other nearby towns would vote for the person they wanted to see run against the probable Democratic candidate, Jerry Voorhis.

Officers in the navy gave Richard permission to travel to California to talk with the Republican leaders in Whittier.

At that meeting, he discussed his views of government.

Throughout the depression years of the 1930s and the years of World War II, the United States had had Democratic presidents, first Franklin Roosevelt and then Harry Truman. Because the depression had left millions of Americans without jobs or enough money to lead a good life, Roosevelt had developed what he called the New Deal. Under the New Deal, many laws were passed to help poor people find jobs, places to live, and other necessities. But the depression ended with World War II, and jobs, both during and after the war, were much easier to find.

Nixon felt that the kind of government developed during the New Deal was no longer needed. Soldiers returning from the war, he told the Republicans in Whittier, were not interested in handouts. Government, he felt, should do what is possible to encourage private companies to hire more people and produce more goods. He felt that the Democratic candidate, Jerry Voorhis, was still thinking in terms of Roosevelt's New Deal, whose time had passed.

After his short speech before the Whittier Republicans, Richard returned to the East and awaited the news from California. A phone call at two o'clock in the morning on November 29 brought the thrilling news. He had easily won their backing for the nomination.

It was an exciting personal victory for Richard, but it was still a long, hard road to become a United States congressman. First, he would have to win the primary election. In that election, voters from California would decide which people would run on Republican, Democratic, and other party tickets. Even if he were to win the primary election, he would still have to face the general election. To become the congressman from his district, he would have to beat the Democratic nominee, probably Jerry Voorhis, who had served in the House of Representatives for many years.

While he was waiting to be released from the navy, Nixon began taking a "crash course" in politics. He studied books and magazine articles about Congress and the people who won elections to that important branch of the federal government. He talked with a number of Republican congressmen to learn more about Jerry Voorhis. And he studied how Jerry Voorhis had voted on every issue to come up in the House of Representatives. He was finally released from the navy in January of 1946, and immediately returned to California to begin his fight to become a congressman.

The Nixons' first daughter, Tricia, was born on February 21 of that year. Even though she was a new mother, Pat managed to find the time to help her husband run his campaign.

The California primary election was held on June 4, 1946. When the votes had been counted, Nixon won the nomination as Republican candidate and, as expected, Jerry Voorhis won for the Democratic side. Despite the victory, Nixon was worried because Voorhis had more total votes than he did. If the same thing happened during the general election in November, the Democrats would be able to send Voorhis back to Congress.

Nixon knew that he would have a tough fight to unseat the Democratic candidate. As the campaign began, it was clear that Voorhis was ahead. But as the contest continued, Richard Nixon began to establish his reputation as one of the toughest political fighters in recent American history.

The debating skills that he had developed in high school and college served him well during the battle for a congressional seat. In a series of debates with Voorhis, Nixon showed that he could organize his thoughts better than the Democratic candidate, and that he remembered the Democrat's voting record better than Voorhis himself could. Nixon embarrassed Voorhis by pointing out that Voorhis had managed to start only one new law in Congress during the last four years. And that law had to do with raising rabbits! Voorhis can do a great job for you in Congress, Richard told his California audiences, if you are a rabbit.

But not all of Richard's attacks against the Democrat were so lighthearted. Nixon pointed out that the New Deal programs of the Democratic government were causing huge national problems. Immediately following the war, there were serious shortages of houses, food, and other goods. All across the country, Republican candidates were asking

Americans if they had "had enough" of Democratic government. Nixon joined the chorus.

But there was an even more important issue that Nixon used to attack Voorhis. The charge itself was simple enough. Voorhis, according to Nixon, was a Communist. As such, he had to be an enemy of the American way of life.

During the 1920s and early 1930s, Jerry Voorhis, like many other Americans, had been a Socialist. Simply stated, Socialists believed that rich people took unfair advantage of working people, forcing the poor to work for low wages while earning fortunes for the wealthy. Most Americans disagreed with the Socialists, but during the height of the depression many also understood the anger Socialists felt when they saw armies of poorly clothed and homeless people searching for work wherever they could find it.

World War II ended the depression, and Russia, a Communist country, helped to end the reign of Adolf Hitler. During the war, America and Russia were allies. Twenty million Russians died defending their homeland against the Nazi invaders. But as soon as the war was over, the Russian government took control of many eastern European countries, including Albania, Bulgaria, Hungary, Poland, and Romania. Early in 1946, the British politician Sir Winston Churchill made a famous speech. In that speech, he warned the world that an "Iron Curtain" had fallen across Europe, and that the countries behind it were enslaved by Russia.

Americans were angered by this turn of events. Socialists, who believed in change through peaceful elections, were lumped together with violent Communists, such as those in power in Russia, in the minds of many Americans. Many people began to fear that Russian Communists would not be satisfied until all the world was Communist. Russian leaders fanned the fears by suggesting that they would soon take over the world.

Richard clearly believed that the Socialist style of the Democratic party was not in the best interests of the United States. He thought Socialists were the same as Communists. Therefore, Jerry Voorhis was a Communist.

When election day finally arrived, Nixon had no idea whether he was ahead or behind in the race. No polls had been taken. Counting the votes proved to be very slow. There were no voting machines in those days. All votes were cast on paper ballots and had to be counted by hand. Not until four o'clock the next morning did he learn the news that he had won. The final count showed that Nixon had received 65,586 votes to 49,994 votes for Voorhis. At the age of thirty-three Richard Nixon had been elected to the United States Congress.

Chapter 3

A CAREER IN THE CAPITAL

On February 18, 1947, Richard and Pat were invited to the White House to meet President Harry S. Truman and the First Lady. The Trumans were having a party to welcome to Washington all the new members of Congress. Richard Nixon was one of them. Also in the group was a newly elected young congressman from Massachusetts named John Fitzgerald Kennedy. Richard wrote that he was impressed by the simple elegance of the White House as well as the kindness of President Truman.

That same day, Nixon made his first speech in the House of Representatives, which, like the smaller Senate, met in the Capitol Building in Washington. In his ten-minute speech, Richard attacked a man named Gerhart Eisler. Eisler was considered a Communist agent by the United States government and had refused to talk with the congressmen. This time, Richard's arguments seemed to have hit their mark. Before long, Eisler fled to East Germany where he became an important official in the Communist government there.

Throughout the year of 1947 Americans were becoming more and more worried about conditions in Europe. The horrible battle scars of World War II were still everywhere on that continent. Many Europeans were left without homes, clothing, and enough food to eat. In France, Italy, and other European countries, the Communist party was telling people that communism was the only political system that could put a stop to the misery created by the war. Americans feared that some countries would soon choose Communist governments.

On July 30, 1947, Nixon was surprised to read in the newspaper that he had been selected to join a group of congressmen to travel to Europe and study the problem first-hand. The Herter Committee, as the group of congressmen was called, set sail aboard the magnificent ocean liner *Queen Mary* at the end of August.

When the congressmen arrived in England, they began to see the terrible conditions that existed there. Many of England's homes and factories had been destroyed by German bombers during the war. Few had been rebuilt. Many people were facing starvation and diseases caused by bad food and poor living conditions.

Traveling on to Germany, the congressmen found that the situation there was even worse. At the end of World War II, the German nation had been divided into two countries. One, East Germany, was controlled by the Russian government. The second, West Germany, was controlled by the United States and a number of European countries. Berlin, which before the war had been a large and beautiful city, was totally destroyed. Three million German citizens were living in the terrible rubble of the bombed-out city. When he visited the ruined headquarters of Adolf Hitler's Nazi government, Nixon was shocked to find starving children trying to sell their fathers' war medals to the wealthy Americans.

In Italy, France, Greece, and other European countries, the Herter Committee found that conditions were almost as bad. In each country he visited, Nixon made a point of meeting with the Communist leaders. He was surprised to find that each Communist he spoke to used the same kind of language to discuss the problems of Europe. Every Communist leader seemed to think the same way that every other Communist did. Nixon decided that all these people must be getting information from Russia, since they spoke in the same terms the Russian leaders used.

A few weeks after they returned to Washington, the congressmen made a number of reports about their trip. Nixon was surprised to learn that most people in and around Whittier, California, did not favor sending aid to Europe. This created a problem for the young congressman. He had been elected to the House of Representatives by the people in the Twelfth Congressional District of California. These people clearly did not want to send huge amounts of money to Europe to help that continent recover from the war.

But everything Nixon saw on his trip made him believe that the aid simply had to be sent. If it were not, he felt certain, millions of Europeans would starve and some countries would be taken over by Communist countries that were stronger. He decided to vote for the aid, and try as best as he could to explain his decision to the voters in California. Many congressmen felt the same way Nixon did. By the end of the year, a huge aid package, called the Marshall Plan, passed the House of Representatives. For several years, the Marshall Plan helped Europeans rebuild their nations, and probably prevented millions of people from starving or becoming Communists. Most of the California citizens eventually agreed with Richard Nixon's decision.

Also in 1947, Nixon became a member of one of the most infamous committees in the history of the House of Representatives. It was called the House Commitee on Un-American Activities, or HUAC for short. The name of this committee would suggest that it was involved in all kinds of activities, but most of its efforts were directed toward investigating possible Communists and Communist organizations in the United States. Although such problems as organized crime and racist organizations might seem to be likely targets for committee investigations, most of the efforts were made against communism.

In August of 1948, an editor for *Time* magazine named Whittaker Chambers appeared before the Un-American

Activities Committee. In the 1920s and 1930s, Chambers had been a member of the Communist party in the United States. By 1938, he had become less interested in helping the Communists and soon decided to leave the party entirely. But, he told the congressmen, before he left, a famous American lawyer named Alger Hiss had given him top secret materials stolen from the United States government. Chambers was suggesting that Alger Hiss was a spy. Many members of the committee were shocked to learn that such a well-known and highly respected American could be involved in illegally helping the Communists.

Then the committee received a telegram from Alger Hiss himself, asking that he be allowed to talk to the congressmen about the charges made against him. When Hiss appeared before the committee on August 5, he said, under oath, that he had never been a member of the Communist party. He also said that he couldn't even remember having met Whittaker Chambers, the man who had accused him of being a Communist spy.

From what both men had said, it was clear that one of them was lying. Many of the congressmen on the committee believed what Alger Hiss said. Hiss was an important lawyer, highly respected by many Americans, including President Harry Truman. Richard Nixon wasn't so sure. Nevertheless, newspaper reporters and government officials, even President Truman, began to accuse the committee of starting a witch-hunt and trying to ruin people's lives unfairly.

This was a very busy time for Congressman Nixon. The Nixons' second daughter, Julie, had been born on July 5, exactly a month before Alger Hiss first appeared before the committee. But even with a newborn infant at home, Nixon decided to make a strong effort to find out which man was telling the truth.

Meeting with Whittaker Chambers, Nixon questioned him at length about Alger Hiss. From the information that Chambers gave, it seemed as if he must have known Hiss. He knew so many personal details about the famous lawyer's life that Nixon began to suspect Hiss was lying when he said he did not remember ever meeting Chambers.

Faced with the problem of how to explain why a man who had never met him could know so much about his personal life, Hiss began to change his story. Now he said that it was possible that Chambers might have lived with him for a short time using a different name. Once again, it was difficult to discover which man was lying.

Alger Hiss might have gotten away with his story. But in the weeks that followed, Whittaker Chambers produced copies of many top secret American papers and Communist party notes, some of them containing notes in the handwriting of Alger Hiss. They virtually proved that Alger Hiss had been both a Communist and a spy. It also proved that Hiss had lied under oath to the committee. Although his activities had occurred too long ago for Hiss to be sent to trial for spying, he was tried for perjury. He was sentenced to five years in jail and served forty-four months before he was released.

Americans were shocked to learn that such a popular lawyer as Alger Hiss had been a Communist spy. The House Un-American Activities Committee, once accused of conducting a witch-hunt, was now praised for its efforts. For his work on the case, Nixon was becoming well known throughout the country, not just in his native California.

But the Hiss affair had another, less positive, result. Because of the surprising investigation, Americans by the millions began to worry that there were Communist spies practically everywhere, especially in government. These fears reached their height during the early 1950s when a number of American politicians, especially Senator Joseph McCarthy of Wisconsin, accused literally thousands of people of being Communist spies. As a result of these charges, the lives of many loyal Americans were upset. The unfair charges were finally stopped in 1954, when the Senate officially stated its dislike for the methods used by McCarthy and his coworkers. By that time, Richard Nixon had become vice-president of the United States and helped to stop the unfair attacks by McCarthy.

All this, however, was many years ahead. In the meantime, Nixon enjoyed the national popularity that the Hiss case had given him. In 1948, he attended the Republican National Convention in Philadelphia where, after a long struggle, Governor Thomas Dewey of New York was chosen to run against the Democratic president, Harry Truman. After the lengthy campaign, most people thought that Dewey would win and that there would be a Republican president for the first time since 1932, when Franklin Roosevelt won his first term in office. But when election day finally arrived later in the year, it was not a good day for Republicans. To nearly everyone's surprise, Truman won the election and the Democrats elected enough people to win a majority in both houses of Congress. For Richard Nixon, the only bright spot was that he had been reelected to the House of Representatives.

The nationwide defeat of the Republican party in the 1948 election gave a hollow ring to Nixon's personal victory in his race for a seat in the House of Representatives. Because of his fame resulting from the Hiss case, he had been much in demand as a campaigner for many Republicans throughout the country. With so many Republicans losing the election, some felt that Nixon had not been an especially good campaigner, although none could deny that he had tried hard.

Also, since the Republican party was now the minority party in the House of Representatives as well as the Senate, Republican congressmen would not have as much power as their Democratic coworkers. Nixon began thinking of himself as a "comer with no place to go." But even if the Republican party seemed to be going nowhere, he reasoned, he might as well try to move up the political ladder on his own.

Nearly as soon as he won reelection to the House of Representatives, Richard Nixon began thinking of the 1950 elections. In that year, voters from California would elect a senator. Although the kind of work that senators and representatives do is quite similar, there are a number of advantages to being a senator. Perhaps most important, senators are elected to terms that are six years long, whereas representatives must face reelection every two years. Also, there are fewer senators than representatives. Senators, therefore, tend to become better known throughout the country. For these reasons, members of the House of Representatives interested in advancing their careers often consider running for the Senate.

In the fall of 1949, Nixon learned that a number of major California newspapers were in favor of his running for a Senate seat. Precisely one year before the election, on November 3, 1949, Nixon announced to a large group of Californians that he intended to run for the Senate. In his speech, he stated what many of his friends and foes alike had already learned from past examples—that he would run a tough, hard-hitting campaign. "There is only one way we can win," he said at the end of his speech. "We must put on a fighting, rocking, socking campaign and carry that campaign directly into every county, city, town, precinct, and home in the state of California."

In the primary elections, Nixon easily won the nomination of his party. Since the Democratic senator from California was retiring, Congresswoman Helen Gahagan Douglas was selected to run on the Democratic ticket. Mrs. Douglas was the wife of a popular Hollywood actor named Melvyn Douglas and had been a noted Broadway star herself during the 1920s. Although Congresswoman Douglas was a popular and attractive figure, Nixon claimed that her record in the House of Representatives showed that she was little more than a secret Communist. His campaign helpers prepared a "fact sheet" about her record, which was printed on pink paper. In those days, "pinko" was a code name for someone who leaned toward the Communist system of government.

Some weeks later, Mrs. Douglas produced her own fact sheet, this time printed on yellow paper. "THE BIG LIE!" the paper began. "Hitler invented it. . . . Nixon uses it. . . . You pick the Congressman the Kremlin loves." It had become a very ugly campaign. A newspaper in San Francisco reported that Mrs. Douglas had called Mr. Nixon "tricky Dick," and that it was Nixon, and not herself, who was playing into the hands of the Communists. The charge was ridiculous, but the name "tricky Dick" would come back to haunt Nixon later in his career.

In fact, many people in Congress felt that Mrs. Douglas's

record was not an especially good one. One particular story shows just how much some members of her own political party disliked Mrs. Douglas.

One afternoon before the campaign had really started, Nixon was working in his congressional office when Congressman John F. Kennedy came to visit him. Kennedy was a Democrat, the same as Mrs. Douglas. When he was seated, he handed Nixon an envelope and said, "Dick, I know you're in for a pretty rough campaign and my father wanted to help out." The envelope contained a check for $1,000. Before he left, the future Democratic president told the future Republican president how he hoped Nixon would defeat Mrs. Douglas, although of course he couldn't say such a thing in public.

When election day arrived, Republican candidates did well over much of the nation. But none did better than Richard Nixon. He collected 680,000 more votes than Douglas. In all, Republicans gained thirty new members in the House of Representatives and five in the Senate, one of whom was, of course, Richard Nixon. In three hard-fought political campaigns, he had yet to lose his first race.

Despite the tremendous effort he had made to become a senator, Mr. Nixon would not keep his new job for very long. There were even bigger things in store for him.

In May of 1951 during a trip to a World Health Organization meeting in Geneva, Switzerland, Senator Nixon was invited to visit General Dwight David Eisenhower at the general's headquarters in Paris. Eisenhower was a tremendously popular person in the United States and in much of Europe. During the closing years of World War II, Eisenhower had been in command of troops from all the countries attempting to defeat Hitler's armies. After the war, he served briefly as the president of Columbia University in New York City, but was soon asked by President Truman to return to the military. When Nixon visited him in Paris, he was in charge of the American and European troops operating under NATO, the North Atlantic Treaty Organization. To millions of people in America and Europe, the general was known affectionately as "Ike."

During their brief meeting, Eisenhower told Nixon that he was impressed by how the congressman had handled the Hiss case. He was also impressed, he said, by many of Nixon's other political speeches and beliefs. For his part, Senator Nixon was impressed by the general's strength of character and understanding of world politics. As the meeting ended, Nixon felt that Ike would make a great president, especially when dealing with foreign affairs.

On July 7 of 1952, Republicans from all over the nation met in Chicago to choose a Republican leader to run for president. Most of the people at this Republican National Convention favored either Senator Robert Taft, the son of former President William Howard Taft, or General Eisenhower. When the votes were taken, Eisenhower won.

Nixon, who was attending the convention, knew that his name had come up as a possible vice-presidential running mate for Eisenhower. He also knew that, in the past, many American vice-presidents had become forgotten men almost as soon as they took office. Few important duties were given to vice-presidents other than presiding over sessions of the Senate and being prepared to take over the presidency if the president should die or become disabled.

After Eisenhower was nominated, Nixon left the convention hall and returned to his hotel room. He really didn't believe that he would be offered the job as Eisenhower's running mate.

It was a hot, summer day in Chicago, and the temperature inside his hotel room was nearly one hundred degrees. Nixon was trying to take a nap when the phone in his room started ringing. An assistant to General Eisenhower was calling.

"We picked you," the caller said simply. "The general asked if you could come see him right away in his suite at the Blackstone Hotel. That is, assuming you want it." Nixon did.

Nixon rushed to the Blackstone Hotel without even taking the time to bathe or shave. As soon as he met the general, he was introduced to Mrs. Eisenhower. The three people spoke for a few minutes and then Mrs. Eisenhower left the room. As soon as she left, the general began discussing his ideas for governing the country. Soon, he asked Nixon if he would be willing to join the campaign.

"I would be proud and happy to," Nixon answered.

"I'm glad you are going to be on the team, Dick," the general continued. "I think that we can win, and I know that we can do the right things for this country." Then, Eisenhower acted as if he had just thought of something. "I just remembered," he said. "I haven't resigned from the army yet."

The general had his secretary help him prepare a letter of resignation. There have probably been many privates in the army who wished they could have resigned so easily. But few could deny that Eisenhower had earned the right to an easy departure.

After talking a little bit longer with Eisenhower, Nixon went directly to the convention hall. Pat Nixon had been having lunch at a Chicago restaurant when she heard the exciting news over the radio. She too went to the convention hall to be with Richard. Since Nixon was clearly Eisenhower's choice for vice-president, nobody was willing to run against him. Nixon was nominated to be the Republican vice-presidental candidate shortly after 6:30 that evening.

As soon as the convention was over and the Nixons returned to Washington, thousands of letters began pouring in to congratulate Nixon as the new Republican vice-presidential nominee. One that Nixon never forgot read as follows:

Dear Dick,

I was tremendously pleased that the convention selected you for V.P. I was always convinced that you would move ahead to the top—but I never thought it would come this quickly. You were an ideal selection and will bring the ticket a great deal of strength.

Please give my best to your wife and all kinds of good luck to you.

Cordially,

Jack Kennedy

But despite all the excitement and praise, both candidates knew that they faced a tough fight to win the election. Today most people running for high national offices use television and radio to get their messages to the American voters. But in 1952, television was still in its infancy. Many families did not own TV sets. Most presidential and vice-presidential candidates toured the country aboard special trains. This kind of exhausting campaigning was called a whistle-stop tour.

With high spirits, Nixon began his whistle-stop tour aboard a train called the Nixon Special leaving from Pomona, a town near Whittier, on September 17, 1952. But the next day, disaster struck!

Nixon had a brief warning that there might be trouble. A

few days earlier, he had been a guest on a well-known Washington broadcast called "Meet the Press." When the show was over, one of the newsmen asked him questions about a large fund of $20,000 a year that was given to Nixon privately by California businessmen, in addition to his regular salary as a senator. Few people knew about this fund until the day after the whistle-stop tour started. Nixon described what happened next in his autobiography, entitled *RN*:

"On September 18, the day after our Pomona kickoff, the fund story exploded across the front page of the late morning edition of the New York *Post*. *Secret Nixon Fund!* the banner screamed; inside another headline said: *Secret Rich Men's Trust Fund Keeps Nixon in Style Far Beyond His Salary.*"

Not surprisingly, Nixon felt that the description was unfair. It was true that a number of California business people had decided to give him what they called "campaign money" throughout his six-year Senate term. But Richard felt that he used the money for fair reasons, such as sending Christmas cards to people who had done volunteer work for him. Many voters wondered, however, how Nixon could speak for all the people of California when he had gotten so much money from a few wealthy businessmen.

Meanwhile, the Democrats had nominated the governor of Illinois, Adlai Stevenson, as their candidate for president. Stevenson and other Democrats began hammering away at the secret contributions. Some even started to demand that Nixon be removed from the Republican ticket.

As the Nixon Special train chugged northward along the West Coast, the story grew into a real crisis. Before long, Nixon learned that editors at the *Washington Post* and *New York Herald Tribune* were calling for him to quit.

A day later, he spoke with General Eisenhower on the phone. The general seemed to be deeply troubled by Nixon's sudden problems. But Eisenhower told his running mate that it should be Nixon's decision, and no one else's, as to whether he should stay in the race. Nixon decided to stay with the campaign and fight the charges against him.

In a series of hasty meetings, Republican leaders decided to put up $75,000 so that Nixon could buy a half hour of television time to answer the charges his critics had made. The broadcast would be made on Tuesday, September 23. In those early days of television, network shows could only be made from New York, Chicago, and Los Angeles. The night before the program, Nixon flew back to Los Angeles. Soon after he arrived, he learned some astounding news!

A Chicago businessman was charging that the Democratic nominee, Adlai Stevenson, had used an almost identical fund as governor of Illinois. Within hours, Stevenson admitted that the charges were true.

Suddenly, Nixon realized that he might be able to survive the charges against him. But the very next day, just hours

52

before he was scheduled to go on national television, there was more bad news. In a telephone call from New York, Tom Dewey, who was the governor of New York and one of Eisenhower's top assistants, said that Nixon should give up the fight. Dewey said that all the other Eisenhower assistants agreed that it was the only answer. Adding insult to injury, Dewey even suggested that Nixon should resign from the Senate as well, and perhaps try again in the next election.

Nixon was shocked. It was only a matter of minutes before he had to leave for the television studio. When he asked if Eisenhower agreed that he should quit, he couldn't get a straight answer. Nixon could only tell Dewey that he didn't have any idea what he would do, and then he hung up.

After a few minutes' thought, he left for the studio. When he arrived, he felt too weak to go through with his prepared speech. Pat stayed by his side, calmed his shattered nerves, and urged him to go through with the broadcast.

As the show began, he felt his confidence gradually return. In his now famous speech, Nixon explained the fund as well as he could, went on to describe how Adlai Stevenson had used a similar fund, and then praised the record and abilities of Eisenhower. He also asked viewers to send letters and telegrams to the Republican National Committee indicating whether he should drop out of the race.

In the speech, Nixon also mentioned that one of the gifts

he had received was a dog named Checkers. He indicated that he had no intention of giving the dog back. To this day, the television broadcast is remembered by many as Nixon's famous "Checkers speech."

Almost all Republicans, and even some Democrats, agreed that Nixon had made a superb speech. Eisenhower, who was campaigning in Cleveland, Ohio, was very impressed. The next day, Eisenhower and Nixon held a private meeting. Although Eisenhower was hearing more rumors about possible scandals that Nixon might be involved in, it was decided that he would stay on the ticket.

During the weeks of campaigning that remained, many other charges were raised against Nixon, especially by some newspaper reporters and, of course, the Democratic candidates. During the campaign, the Nixons traveled 46,000 miles, visiting 214 cities and making ninety-two major speeches. In the end, General Eisenhower's popularity and Nixon's skill at public speaking won out over the many charges leveled against the vice-presidential candidate. When the election day votes were counted, the Eisenhower-Nixon ticket won by a whopping 6.5 million votes.

At the relatively young age of thirty-nine, Richard Nixon had been elected to the second highest office in the land. The job was a heartbeat away from the presidency. But the road to that high office had not been an easy one. In the future, it would become even more difficult.

Chapter 4

MR. VICE-PRESIDENT

On January 20, 1953, Richard Nixon took the oath of office for the vice-presidency of the United States. Hannah Nixon brought to Washington two Bibles that had been in her family for many years for use in the ceremony. For the first time in two decades, a Republican president and vice-president had been elected by the American people.

For Vice-President Nixon, the most fascinating part of his first year in office was a trip to Asia that Eisenhower had asked him to make in the fall. The vice-president and Pat Nixon started on the long trip on October 5, 1953. It would be more than two months before the couple returned to the United States. Pat especially was sad that she would be far away from her daughters, Tricia and Julie, for such a long time.

Before the trip had started, the vice-president had insisted that the visits be scheduled so that he could meet as many different kinds of people as possible. It was an unusual request. Usually, American officials visiting foreign countries spoke only to political leaders and other influential people. Nixon felt he would learn more about the Asian nations if he could speak with people from all walks of life.

After stopovers in New Zealand and Australia, the vice-president's plane flew to the first Asian stop, Jakarta, Indonesia. "We were greeted by President Sukarno," Nixon later wrote in his autobiography, "whose tastes were as rich as his people were poor." One night during the visit, the Nixons ate dinner served on golden plates under the light of a thousand torches. But beyond the Indonesian palace, many of the country's people were facing starvation.

The Nixons spent six days visiting the countries of French Indochina—Cambodia, Laos, and Vietnam. Although these three countries were supposedly ruled by France, Communist soldiers were fighting to drive the French out. In Vietnam especially, Nixon sensed that the French soldiers and politicians there had little love for the Asian people. Visiting French and Vietnamese soldiers fighting fierce battles against the Communists, he could see what little effort the French made to gain the friendship of the Vietnamese soldiers. Nevertheless, he felt that only the French army stood between Indochina and certain takeover by the Communists. He knew that the French were behaving badly, but he felt that they had to be encouraged to stay and fight against the Communists.

From Indochina the Nixons flew on to South Korea. Until just a few months before his trip, the country of Korea had been involved in a fierce war. As in Indochina, Communists had been fighting non-Communists. The United States had sent many soldiers to help battle the Communists. Somewhat later, China sent even more soldiers to fight against the Americans and other non-Communist troops. Finally, a peace treaty was signed that divided Korea into two nations. North Korea was ruled by a Communist government. South Korea was governed by non-Communists.

The president of South Korea, Syngman Rhee, was very unhappy to see his nation split into two countries and was threatening to start the war once again. Eisenhower had asked Nixon to convince the South Korean president to promise not to fight anymore. Rhee was very reluctant to make such a promise. He finally said that he would send Eisenhower a letter promising not to do anything without the support of the United States.

When the Nixons flew to Japan, they became the first official representatives of another government to visit Japan since World War II. Large crowds of Japanese cheered the Americans wherever they went. In Japan, the vice-president made a speech saying that the Japanese should be allowed to organize an army once again. Many people throughout the world were against such action. The horrible memories of World War II were still too fresh. But Nixon felt that Japan would someday have to defend itself against Communist Russia or China, and that an army would be needed.

Of all the countries he visited, Nixon was most fascinated by Burma, which had recently won its independence from

Britain. When the Nixons drove into the Burmese jungle to see a famous religious statue, they were warned that there would be anti-American demonstrations staged by the Communists. Richard made a point of meeting the Communist demonstrators and talking with them.

Before he flew back to the United States, the vice-president visited India, Pakistan, and Iran, where he spoke to each country's leaders. In India he was disappointed to discover that Prime Minister Jawaharlal Nehru, the country's leader, wanted only to talk about how much he hated the people of Pakistan. No other issue seemed to concern him. When Nixon visited Pakistan, he found little love for India there.

On December 14, 1953, the plane carrying the Nixons arrived back at National Airport in Washington, D.C. After driving to the city the Nixons had coffee with the Eisenhowers. The next day, Ike sent a note saying how much he appreciated the Nixons' efforts to make the long trip a success.

Nixon enjoyed reading reports about his trip in newspapers from the countries he visited. Many of the foreign reporters said that they were very surprised that an American vice-president would take the time to visit and talk with common farmers and factory workers. It was great fun to read such reports, but the visit had filled Nixon with worry for the future of many of the nations he visited.

For some time, many of the nations of Asia had been colonies of European countries and were governed by Europeans. Nearly all of these Asian countries wanted to be independent and free of European rule. But as the Europeans began to leave, would the countries become Communist or non-Communist? To the vice-president, it seemed as if only the European governors were keeping many countries from becoming Communist. And the Europeans themselves often were not good advertisements for democracy.

In his autobiography, Nixon described a conversation he had with an Oriental leader who lived on the island of Hong Kong, near mainland China. For some years the island city had been ruled by the British, who had helped give Hong Kong probably the strongest economy in all of Asia.

"How would the people of Hong Kong vote if the British offered them independence?" Nixon asked a political leader there.

"They would vote for independence by ten to one," the answer came immediately. The vice-president asked how this could be so, when the people had so obviously been helped by British rule.

"There is a saying that when the British established a colony," the Oriental man replied, "they built three things, in this order: a church, a racetrack, and a club to which Orientals cannot belong. . . . That is why we would always choose to be independent."

The vice-president realized that although Europeans were

keeping a number of Asian nations from becoming Communist, their lack of respect for Asian people might eventually allow the Communists to have the upper hand. With his obvious concern about communism, it is odd that, upon his return to the United States, Nixon was asked by Eisenhower to help stop the wild, anti-Communist crusades of Senator Joseph McCarthy. Senator McCarthy's vicious attacks against many Americans he thought were Communists greatly angered President Eisenhower. In the long battle to oust the senator from power, Nixon was forced to criticize a man he personally liked. But he also knew that Senator McCarthy had acted too harshly. When the Senate decided to form a committee to criticize McCarthy and point out his errors, a freshman senator named Sam Ervin was put in charge of the group. Years later, Sam Ervin would do much to end the political career of Richard Nixon.

In March of 1954, one of the vice-president's greatest fears resulting from his trip to Asia came to pass. A French fort at Dien Bien Phu in Vietnam was on the verge of being overrun by Communist soldiers. As newspapers reported the increasingly desperate situation faced by the French on a day-to-day basis, some American military officers suggested using atomic bombs against the Communist Vietnamese soldiers. Instead, Eisenhower decided to send a small group of two hundred American soldiers to Vietnam to help fight the Communists. It was the start of American involvement in the Vietnam War. Increasing numbers of American troops would be sent to Vietnam for nearly twenty years.

On May 7, 1954, the hopelessly outnumbered French soldiers at Dien Bien Phu were overrun by Communist troops. Shortly after the defeat, the French decided to give up the fight in Vietnam. On July 21 at a peace conference in Geneva, Switzerland, it was decided that the nation of Vietnam would be divided into two new countries. North Vietnam would be governed by Communists, South Vietnam by non-Communists. President Eisenhower and Vice-President Nixon did not wish to see half the nation taken over by a Communist government. So the United States, even though it had several hundred troops in the Asian country, did not sign the peace agreement.

In the years that followed, Nixon and other members of the United States government would try to talk a number of other countries into helping in the fight against Vietnamese Communists. But not everyone was willing to help. The famous British statesman Sir Winston Churchill, for example, felt that it would not be worth the terrible fighting to keep the Communists from taking over in the faraway nation. On the other hand, many Americans, including the president and vice-president, felt differently. Nixon feared that if Vietnam were lost, many other countries might fall to the Communists as well, just like a row of dominoes falling down after the first one has been tipped.

But there were many other matters to think about besides Vietnam. In the elections of 1954, Americans voted on candidates for the House of Representatives. They also voted on one third of the Senate seats. Nixon worked hard to get Republicans elected to Congress. But despite his efforts, Democrats gained a majority in both the House and the Senate.

The news from the 1954 elections was not particularly good for Republicans, but an event the following year was even worse. On the evening of September 24, 1955, Nixon was reading a copy of a Washington newspaper. The paper reported that President Eisenhower was suffering from indigestion. Richard Nixon thought little of the story since the president often suffered from an upset stomach. But then the phone rang.

"Dick, this is Jim Hagerty," an aide for the president said over the phone. "I have some bad news—the president has had a coronary."

"Are you sure?" Nixon asked.

"We are absolutely sure," the presidential aide replied. "Dick," the voice continued, "let me know where you can be reached at all times." Nixon knew exactly what those worrisome words meant. If President Eisenhower should die, Richard Nixon would immediately become president of the United States. With little or no notice, he would be in full command of America's defense forces, as well as many other parts of the federal government.

President Eisenhower survived his serious illness. But for nearly two months while he was in a hospital, Nixon had to perform many of the president's duties. When Eisenhower returned to his work in Washington in November, thousands of people cheered in the streets as his car moved toward the White House.

As soon as the president returned to the White House, it was time to think about the 1956 elections, which were about a year away. Eisenhower had to think seriously about whether to run for a second term as president. His wife was against it. She feared that four more years of the difficult job might lead to another heart attack. After much thought, at a meeting with reporters on February 29, 1956, Eisenhower finally announced his decision to run again.

At the same meeting, a reporter asked if Eisenhower wanted to keep Nixon as his vice-president. Ike answered that, although he admired the vice-president very much, he would wait to see whom the Republican party nominated for the job. Nixon must have been disappointed at the president's answer. By not wholeheartedly supporting his vice-president, Eisenhower's remarks caused a few Republicans to begin a "dump Nixon" campaign. Fortunately for Nixon, the campaign was far from successful. When the Republican party met in August to nominate its candidates, Nixon was selected to be Eisenhower's running mate by a vote of 1,323 to 1.

Despite the good news, the summer of 1956 was not a happy time for Richard Nixon. During the Republican Convention in August, he learned that his father was seriously ill. While Eisenhower made a speech to cheering Republicans at the convention in San Francisco, Nixon was four hundred miles south, staying by his father's bedside in Whittier. Frank Nixon died on September 4, 1956.

As Richard Nixon knew better than almost anyone, national politics left little time for personal grief. Just two weeks after his father's death, Nixon began his first campaign trip to convince American voters to elect Eisenhower and himself to a second term in office. On the morning of September 18, President Eisenhower traveled to Washington's National Airport to wish Mr. and Mrs. Nixon a good trip.

Eight years earlier, in 1948, Harry Truman campaigned for the presidency to cries of "Give 'em hell" from his supporters. In 1956, Ike told Nixon to "Give 'em heaven" during his trip. It is easy to understand why the president spoke these words.

In 1956, nearly all Americans were enjoying good times. The economy was very strong and jobs were easy to find. By the millions, Americans were buying their own homes in the nation's suburbs, buying new cars every few years, and enjoying the benefits of the richest country on earth. Although a few hundred American soldiers were advising the non-Communist troops in Vietnam, for the most part America was at peace. World War II and the more recent Korean War were nearly forgotten.

Once again, the Democrats nominated Adlai Stevenson to run against the popular Republican president. But Eisenhower and Nixon could accurately say that, under Republican leadership in the 1950s, Americans had never had it so good.

By the year 1956, television had become an important force in American life—nearly three quarters of American homes had at least one television set. For the first time in history, Richard Nixon used television as a major tool in a political campaign. On October 4, he made a live nationwide broadcast during which questions were asked by reporters in eight different cities. He would continue to use television until his final campaign in 1972. But in 1956, the Nixons also traveled on three major cross-country campaign trips.

When election day arrived, the Republican ticket of Eisenhower and Nixon scored a major victory. But once again, Republicans lost in Congress. Democrats controlled both the House and the Senate.

More than any other vice-president in history, Nixon took an active role in governing the country. Almost exactly a year after the 1956 elections, President Eisenhower once again became seriously ill, this time suffering a stroke. Again, Nixon had to take over many of the duties of the president.

Throughout much of his political life, Nixon had become increasingly well known as a tough anti-Communist. Because of the extremes some anti-Communists, especially Senator Joseph McCarthy, had gone to, Americans were realizing that some anti-Communist activities could be dangerous. But during his second term as vice-president, a number of events throughout the world showed that Americans did, indeed, have reason to fear the uncontrolled spread of communism.

In 1956, many people in Hungary, a country in central Europe, started fighting against the rule of their own Communist government. Just when it appeared that they might win, tanks and armed soldiers from Communist Russia invaded Hungary. Many of the anti-Communist fighters were killed and others were put in prison. The Russians then changed some of the ways Hungarians were governed, making it very unlikely that the Hungarian people would ever be able to change their government.

In December of 1956, Nixon traveled to Austria, where he saw some of the thousands of Hungarians who had fled their homes trying to escape the Russian troops. In all, more than 100,000 Hungarians left their homes and most of their possessions to escape the cruel Russian invasion. In Austria,

Nixon saw firsthand how the Hungarian refugees were suffering, depending on the Red Cross for food and shelter. He also learned that many of the Hungarian refugees blamed the United States, in part, for their problems. In the months and days before the revolt, Radio Free Europe and the Voice of America—democratic radio broadcasts aimed at people behind the Iron Curtain—had urged the Hungarians to fight against their government. When they did, the United States did nothing to prevent a massacre as the Russians invaded to put down the revolt.

The problems created by violent Communists soon began to appear closer to America's borders. In 1958 Vice-President Nixon began a tour of South America, a continent much closer to the United States than faraway Europe and Asia. None of the countries in South America was governed by Communists, but most South American countries were not democracies, either. Many of these nations were ruled by small groups of people, often headed by one powerful leader called a dictator. In almost every South American country, it was against the law to be a Communist.

Nevertheless, during his trip south, Nixon found large groups of people, often led secretly by Communists, who were angry at the United States. In Uruguay, Argentina, Paraguay, and Bolivia, the numbers of people shouting angry threats at the Nixons were relatively small. Many other people cheered the Americans. But in Peru, the situation got much worse. There, huge groups of people shouted, in Spanish, words like "Nixon go home!" and even "Death to Nixon!" One group of demonstrators even began throwing rocks at the Americans, who were forced to leave without talking to the angry crowd.

The angry crowds and ugly words the Nixons saw and heard in Peru were frightening enough. In Venezuela the Americans were nearly killed. As the Nixons' cars drove into the city of Caracas, their driver had to speed past dozens of rocks thrown from the side of the road. But when they arrived near the center of the city, a row of parked cars blocked the street. The driver was forced to stop.

Suddenly, hundreds of people began running toward the stopped automobile. The Venezuelan policemen drove away on their motorcycles as soon as the angry mob began advancing toward the vice-president's car. Soon, the car windows were being smashed by rocks and splinters of glass were crashing all around the people inside. A man with an iron pipe in his hand began smashing the front windshield. Nixon was looking at the car behind him in which Pat was riding. She seemed to be safe, but suddenly his own car began rocking back and forth.

The angry mob was trying to overturn his car! Overturned, it would be easy to set the gasoline tank on fire. For the first time on his trip, Nixon thought he might be killed. But then at the last moment, the car in front of him managed to break through the crowds and parked cars, and began speeding away from the angry mob.

The Nixons were safe, but the experience was frightening. Several people in the vice-president's car had been badly cut by shattered glass. That afternoon, Nixon told reporters in Caracas that the mobs had been led by Communists. Communists throughout the world, he said, were attempting to destroy the United States and the American way of life. Back in the United States, Americans were shocked to learn the news that many people in South America seemed to hate them. President Eisenhower even became alarmed. Before the shocking news even reached the American public, he put a large number of army and marine troops on alert, in case the Nixons' group needed to be rescued.

It is unlikely that all the angry South Americans were Communists. Some may simply have been jealous of the wealth and power of the United States. Others may have been angered that the United States government seemed to support anyone in South America who was anti-Communist, even if the ruler happened to be a cruel dictator. But little more than a year after his trip to the South American continent, another event brought the very real threat of communism to within ninety miles off the coast of Florida.

On New Year's Day in 1959, the troops of Fidel Castro entered the streets of Havana, the capital of the island nation of Cuba. The government of Fidel Castro eventually replaced the cruel dictatorship of non-Communist President Fulgencio Batista. But in the months and years that followed Castro's victory, it became clear to the Americans that Castro was a Communist. Within just a few years, Castro would try to bring Russian nuclear missles to Cuba, within easy range of Washington, D.C., and other American cities.

Later that year, on July 22, Richard and Pat Nixon left for a visit to Russia, the heart of the Communist world. When the vice-president's airplane arrived in Moscow, the capital of Russia, there were no crowds to meet him. A Russian official gave a long welcoming speech, but Nixon knew that he was not being welcomed as a great friend of the Russian government.

The next day, the American vice-president had his first meeting with Russian Premier Nikita Khrushchev. The long talk between the two world leaders was not a friendly one. Khrushchev was angry because both Eisenhower and Nixon had suggested that the people of Communist nations were slaves. The Russian leader also suggested that the United States seemed to want to destroy every Communist country in the world. Before long, the two men were using harsh insults in an attempt to shock each other.

President Eisenhower had asked his vice-president to go to Russia to attend an exhibit of American life and products that was being held in Moscow. As Nixon and Khrushchev arrived at the exhibit, the arguments broke out again.

Pointing to a Russian worker helping to set up the exhibit, Khrushchev asked, "Does this man look like a slave laborer? With men of such spirit, how can we lose?"

"With men like that, *we* are strong!" said Nixon, pointing to an American worker at the same exhibit. "But these men," Nixon continued, "Soviet and American, work together well for peace, even as they have worked together in building this exhibition. This is the way it should be. . . . There must be a free exchange of ideas. You must not be afraid of ideas. After all, you don't know everything."

"If *I* don't know everything," the Russian replied with anger, "*you* don't know anything about communism, except fear of it!" It was obvious that these two world leaders would not be able to solve the problems between their two countries. Yet, as Nixon had learned from many different people all over the world, even the harshest of political enemies could enjoy moments of friendship. But during his visit to Russia, most friendly moments were brief. Before long, even the most polite conversation turned to the political problems between democratic and Communist countries.

When they returned home in early August, the Nixons found a large crowd cheering them at the airport. Films had been made—and shown on American television—of Nixon's talk with Khrushchev at the American exhibition in Moscow. To many American television viewers, Nixon was immediately seen as the man who stood up to the fierce Russian leader, Nikita Khrushchev.

With the year 1959 rapidly drawing to a close, many American politicians were already beginning to think of the 1960 presidential elections. Having served two terms, Eisenhower could not run for a third. As Eisenhower's vice-president, Nixon knew that he had a good chance at being nominated as the Republican candidate for president. He would win the nomination and run against a brash senator from Massachusetts in the closest presidential election in American history.

A photo of the Nixon family: first row, Donald (on his mother's lap) and Richard; second row: Harold and Hannah; standing, Frank Nixon

Above: Richard Nixon as a member of the Whittier football team wears number 12.
Below: Richard Nixon entered the navy in 1942 as a lieutenant (jg) and was a lieutenant commander when he was discharged.

Above: Louis Russell and Representative Richard Nixon confer at the Hiss-Chambers hearing in August of 1948.
Below: Vice-President and Mrs. Richard Nixon are shown leaving the Imperial Palace in Tokyo.

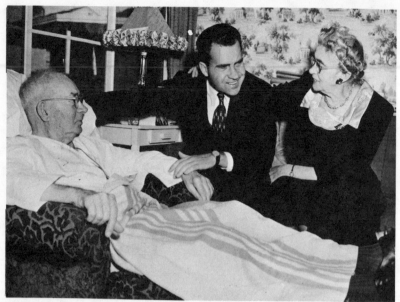

Above: In 1954 Vice-President Nixon returned to Whittier, California, to visit his father, who was ill, and his mother.
Below: On a tour of Russia in 1959, Nikita Khrushchev stands next to Richard Nixon while Mrs. Khrushchev is on Mrs. Nixon's left.

Above: President Lyndon Johnson and President-elect Richard Nixon talk to reporters after Johnson had briefed Nixon on foreign policy. Below: Henry A. Kissinger, President-elect Richard M. Nixon, and the Amir of Kuwait meet in December of 1968.

Above: As Mrs. Nixon looks on, Richard M. Nixon takes the oath of office as the thirty-seventh president. Administering the oath is Chief Justice Earl Warren. Behind him is outgoing President Johnson.

Below: On Father's Day of 1969, President Nixon poses with his daughters, Julie Nixon Eisenhower (left) and Tricia, in the Rose Garden of the White House.

Above: President Nixon works over problems of the United States and the world in his office in 1971.
Below: During a cabinet meeting in the White House in August of 1974, President Nixon talks about his involvement in the Watergate cover-up to Secretary of State Henry Kissinger (left) and Defense Secretary James Schlesinger.

Chapter 5

NO ROOM AT THE WHITE HOUSE

In 1960, both the Democratic and Republican parties held their national conventions in July. At their convention the Democrats selected the handsome young senator from the state of Massachusetts, John Fitzgerald Kennedy. His vice-presidential running mate was an older man, the Democratic Senate leader from Texas, Lyndon Johnson.

At the Republican National Convention less than two weeks later, Richard Nixon easily won his party's nomination for president. Both the Republican leaders at the convention and Vice-President Nixon himself favored Henry Cabot Lodge, the United States representative to the United Nations, for vice-president. With the nominations complete, Nixon knew that there would be four tough months of campaigning before the elections in November.

In terms of experience, the Republican nominee knew that he had a great advantage over the popular young senator from Massachusetts. Nixon had served as an active vice-president for nearly eight years. Because President Eisenhower had a number of major illnesses while serving in office, Nixon had already assumed many of the duties of a president. In his role as vice-president, Nixon had attended many sessions of the Senate and was familiar with many of the new laws being considered in the United States. As a well-traveled spokesman for America, he also had a good understanding of foreign problems and opportunities.

But John F. Kennedy also had a number of advantages. Although it shouldn't matter, Kennedy was a very handsome man. His good looks, Nixon knew, would help Kennedy when he appeared on television. In addition, the Massachusetts senator had the ability to make people laugh, and a sense of humor was never one of Nixon's strong points. Like Nixon, Senator Kennedy was a superb public speaker who had fine-tuned his debating skills not only in Congress, but earlier at Harvard University, probably the most highly respected college in the United States. Finally, Kennedy was a Catholic. No Catholic had ever been a United States president, and some people thought that his religion might hurt Kennedy in the election. But Nixon felt that it might help him. Some people, he thought, might vote for Kennedy simply because they thought it was time for a Catholic to become president.

By 1960, television was well on its way to becoming the most popular source of entertainment in the nation. Almost everyone had a television set. Both candidates knew that television would be the most important tool available for winning the presidency, and both were determined to take advantage of it.

For the first time in history, the presidential candidates agreed to a series of face-to-face debates that would be nationally televised. The four debates took place in September and October of 1960, a matter of weeks before the election. More than ever before, television brought a presidential campaign into the living rooms of Americans all across the nation.

Both candidates were very skilled debaters. After the final debate ended on October 21, many viewers felt it was almost impossible to say exactly who won. But nearly everyone could agree on one thing: there was no question that Kennedy *looked* better than Nixon. In the first debate, especially, Nixon had been ill and was ten pounds underweight. The collar of his shirt hung too loosely around his neck and his skin was pale. By contrast, Kennedy was tanned and healthy looking.

During the debates Kennedy hammered away at the record of President Eisenhower, which he felt was not a particularly good one. The most famous complaint that Kennedy made was that Eisenhower had allowed a "missile gap" to develop between the United States and Russia. Eisenhower, he said, had allowed the Russians to build far more nuclear missiles than the United States. America, he suggested, was no longer safe.

Like many Democrats, Kennedy believed in a government that took an active role in developing the economy of the nation. True to the Republican spirit, Nixon believed that government should pretty much leave business and industry alone, interfering only when great problems arose that only the federal government could solve.

In the four long debates, the two masterful politicians developed many other issues, of course. But after all the speeches were over, the debates seemed to change very few opinions among American voters. Before the debates began, public opinion polls gave Senator Kennedy a tiny lead over Vice-President Nixon. After the final debate, the polls still gave Kennedy a slight lead, but this time it was even smaller. Because polls are not completely accurate, most people agreed that the race was too close to call.

After the last debate, only two weeks were left before the election. If he were to win, Nixon knew, he would have to campaign extremely hard. But he also knew that he had a secret weapon. Dwight Eisenhower, who was serving the last few months of his final term in office, was one of the most popular presidents in American history. Eisenhower had been greatly angered by Kennedy's attacks on his policies, and especially by his suggestion that there was a so-called missile gap. He knew full well that no missile gap existed, and he was anxious to get out on the campaign trail to help his vice-president win the November election.

But at the last minute, both Eisenhower's wife and his doctor called Nixon to explain that the president's health was so poor that the campaign might kill him. Nixon urged Eisenhower to make just a few speeches in his favor. He knew that he had lost a valuable weapon in his quest for the nation's highest office.

When election day finally arrived, about seventy million Americans cast their votes for president. It was an extraordinarily close election, the closest presidential vote since 1888. Nixon watched the results on television from his headquarters in Los Angeles. By midnight, Kennedy had a slight lead, but it was still very close. For some reason, votes from the city of Chicago and some areas of the state of Texas were very late coming in.

Without knowing who won, Nixon finally went to sleep. In the middle of the night, Senator Kennedy called the mayor of Chicago, Richard J. Daley, and asked him how the voting results were coming. According to Benjamin Bradlee, editor of the *Washington Post* newspaper, Mayor Daley said, "Mr. President, with a little bit of luck and the help of a few close friends, you're going to carry Illinois."

The next day, it was clear that Kennedy did indeed carry the state of Illinois. When Nixon was awakened by his daughter Julie at six o'clock in the morning, the vote was even closer than it had been the night before. But as the day continued, it was finally obvious that Kennedy had won by the small margin of 100,000 votes.

For the first time since he was in school, Richard Nixon

had lost an election. Many politicians feared that some votes may have been stolen, or invented, in Chicago and Texas. But Nixon knew that to challenge the election would take months of work and a great deal of money. Still, many people, Republicans and Democrats alike, have openly wondered whether Kennedy or Nixon really collected the most votes in the election of 1960.

On January 20, 1961, Nixon's second term as vice-president of the United States was completed. John F. Kennedy would replace Dwight Eisenhower in the White House, and Lyndon Johnson would be the new vice-president. The day after Kennedy became president, Mr. and Mrs. Nixon flew to the Bahamas for a vacation. The couple decided that Pat would remain in Washington while Tricia and Julie finished the school year there, and Richard would return to California to seek work with a law firm. When school was completed, Pat and the kids would join Richard in California.

Before long, the former vice-president found work with a law firm in Los Angeles. But for a man who had spent almost his entire adult life in public office, returning to private practice was difficult.

Almost as soon as he returned to California, friends began suggesting that Nixon run for governor of California in the 1962 elections. Among the people who urged him to do so was Dwight Eisenhower, who, in a visit to the California resort town of Palm Springs, suggested that the governorship of California would be a good starting point for another run for the presidency.

On September 27, 1961, Nixon held a meeting with reporters in California. There he announced that he would run for governor of California on the Republican ticket. He also said that he would not be a candidate for president in 1964. John Kennedy, he felt, would be very difficult to defeat.

Around the same time, he was working on his first book, called *Six Crises*. In that book, Nixon told how a number of particularly difficult situations, in both private and public life, had helped to shape his character.

Although he easily won the Republican nomination in the June primary elections, he lost badly in the general elections to the Democratic candidate, Pat Brown.

Richard Nixon lost the California election by nearly 300,000 votes, a large margin for a state election. All across the nation, reporters were saying that Nixon was finished in politics. The former vice-president did little to help his own case. When it was clear that he had lost the California election, he met with reporters in California and gave one of the most surprising speeches in the history of American politics. In part, here is what he said:

"And as I leave the press, all I can say is this: for sixteen years, ever since the Hiss case, you've had a lot of—a lot of fun—that you've had an opportunity to attack me, and I think I've given as good as I've taken.

"I leave you gentlemen now and you will now write it. You will interpret it. That's your right. But as I leave you I want you to know—just think how much you're going to be missing.

"You won't have Nixon to kick around anymore, because, gentlemen, this is my last press conference. . . ." Nixon continued with his angry speech, but the remainder of his talk was not so shocking. What was more alarming was his appearance. Unshaven and exhausted from yet another tough campaign, he hardly looked like a man who, just two years earlier, had held the second highest office in the land. And not only would this not be his last press conference, but tragically, in a few years the press would "kick him around" until he was out of the White House.

After his bitter defeat in the 1962 election, there was little to keep Richard Nixon and his family in California. Shortly after the election, the Nixons moved to New York City. The two Nixon children, Julie and Tricia, were particularly excited about the idea of living in the nation's largest city. But for the former vice-president, the thought of once again settling into a career as a lawyer in New York must have been hard to accept.

From the time of his defeat in the 1960 presidential campaign, Richard Nixon was out of office for eight years. But if this was a difficult time for him, it was an even harder time for America.

On November 20, 1963, Nixon flew to Dallas, Texas, to meet with officials from the Pepsi-Cola company, who did business with his New York law firm. Driving toward the Dallas airport to begin his flight home on November 22, he saw American flags all along the roads to the airport. President John F. Kennedy was due to arrive in Dallas within the hour. Shortly after his airplane arrived in New York, Nixon heard the terrible news that the American president had been shot dead by a gunman. Lyndon Johnson was the new president of the United States.

In April of 1964, Nixon traveled to South Vietnam as a private citizen. But, as always during his travels, he was followed by reporters anxious to talk to the former vice-president. In Saigon, the capital of South Vietnam, Nixon learned that the war in Vietnam, despite increasing numbers of United States troops present, was going badly for the non-Communists.

That summer, he attended the Republican National Convention in San Francisco. There, the Republicans nominated Senator Barry Goldwater to be their candidate for president. Nixon gave a short speech introducing Goldwater to the cheering Republicans.

Goldwater would run against the Democratic president, Lyndon Johnson, who had succeeded as president when Kennedy was killed. Although Goldwater seemed to be a likable and honest man, he ran a very poor campaign. At one point, he suggested that even low-ranking military officers should be allowed to use nuclear weapons in the field. Lyndon Johnson won the election by a landslide.

As president in his first term, Lyndon Johnson greatly increased the number of American soldiers fighting against the Communists in South Vietnam. As the war dragged on, more and more Americans began to oppose sending American soldiers to fight and die in a country so far away. And more Americans began to distrust their own government. All across the nation, young people, especially college students, began to protest against the war in Vietnam. As the end of his first term grew near, President Johnson found that the Vietnamese war was the single most important issue in American politics. His plans for a "Great Society" in America, and all his other ideas, were overshadowed by the unpopular war.

When, near the end of 1966, Richard Nixon decided to try again to become president of the United States in the 1968 elections, America was becoming a deeply divided nation. More and more people were beginning to protest *against* the war, and *for* the civil rights of American blacks and other minorities. On college campuses and in major cities, demonstrations were growing larger.

To prepare himself for another hard campaign, Nixon decided to make a major world trip in 1967. In the trips he had made around the world as vice-president, he had always talked with officials at the Central Intelligence Agency (CIA) before leaving. This time he tried to do the same, but learned that President Johnson had given orders for no one at the CIA to talk with him. Johnson had been angered by some of Nixon's speeches against his peace efforts in Vietnam.

Although he was without the valuable information the CIA could have given him, Nixon nevertheless made a successful trip to Europe, Asia, and South America. He had valuable talks with some of the leaders who had known him as vice-president, as well as a number of new leaders. But as always, he made an attempt to talk with ordinary people as well as important politicians.

Upon his return to New York on June 24, Nixon found that his support for a presidential bid was growing, although some people were concerned that he might be thought of as a "loser" after his defeat in California. In the fall, he visited nearly all the Republican governors and party leaders in their home states.

Just as he was beginning to get his campaign in full swing, he heard some sad news from California. His brother Don called to say that their mother, Hannah Nixon, had just died. In his autobiography, Richard Nixon wrote lovingly of his mother, who had spent much of her life struggling to keep the members of her family alive and well.

Despite the heartache, Nixon knew that he had little time left to begin his campaign for the presidency. America, it seemed, was coming apart at the seams. Huge demonstrations against the Vietnam War were going on all across the nation. Lyndon Johnson was becoming more and more unpopular in the eyes of American voters.

The first Republican primary election would be held, as usual, in the state of New Hampshire. The winner there would have a good head start in the race for the nomination. Nixon officially began his campaign with a meeting with reporters in New Hampshire on February 2, 1968. His first words were, "Gentlemen, this is *not* my last press conference."

When the primary election was held, Nixon won the state of New Hampshire by a landslide. In the same state, the Democratic voters cast their votes narrowly in favor of the current Democratic president, Lyndon Johnson. Surprisingly, receiving almost as many Democratic votes was the strong anti-war candidate Eugene McCarthy.

The close Democratic race was a great embarrassment for Lyndon Johnson. Shortly after that first primary election, President Johnson announced that he would not run for a second term as president. Another primary was held in Wisconsin on April 2. Richard Nixon and Eugene McCarthy easily won the support of their two parties.

Two days later, terrible news came out of Memphis, Tennessee. The Reverend Martin Luther King, Jr., the brilliant spokesman for millions of black Americans seeking justice in their own land, was shot dead. Almost immediately, riots broke out in Washington, New York, Chicago, Boston, Detroit, and elsewhere. To the anger of the largely young and white antiwar protesters was added the fury of hundreds of thousands of black people, who now felt there was little hope left. America, it seemed, could not stand another crisis, but more were to come.

Nixon and McCarthy continued to win in the state primary elections. But somewhat late in the campaign, Bobby Kennedy, brother of the slain President Kennedy, announced that he would run for the Democratic nomination for president. When the important California primary election was held, Nixon's nomination seemed nearly certain. But on the Democratic ticket, Kennedy defeated Eugene McCarthy. For a few hours, Nixon thought that he would once again be running against a Kennedy.

Right after his victory speech, however, Bobby Kennedy was shot dead by a lone gunman. Yet another Kennedy had been slain, and yet another tragedy overcame a nation reeling from many other crises. America was at war in Vietnam, and seemed to be at war with itself as well. Lyndon Johnson, who had declared that he would not run again, was becoming an increasingly unpopular president. The nation desperately needed new leadership.

When the Republican National Convention met in August,

Nixon was fairly certain that he had the votes to win the nomination. But at the last minute, two powerful governors, Nelson Rockefeller of New York and Ronald Reagan of California, joined forces to try to take the nomination away from him. When the votes of the Republican leaders were counted, Nixon won by a bare margin of twenty-five. Ronald Reagan then asked everyone to vote for Nixon on a second ballot, to make the vote unanimous. Once again, Richard Nixon was the Republican candidate for president.

The Democratic National Convention was held in Chicago, and quickly became a total disaster. Although Eugene McCarthy's strong antiwar campaign had given him a great many votes, the Democrats nominated Hubert Humphrey, who was Lyndon Johnson's vice-president. Believing that the nomination was being stolen from the antiwar candidate Eugene McCarthy, tens of thousands of mostly young people gathered in Chicago to protest the Democratic Convention. Untrained in how to deal with such large numbers of protesters, members of the Chicago Police Department rioted, attacking unarmed demonstrators with billy clubs, nightsticks, and tear gas.

The Democratic party was badly hurt by the disaster in Chicago. It was also hurt by the unpopular war in Vietnam. Although the Republican President Dwight Eisenhower had sent the first American soldiers there, the Democratic presidents John Kennedy and especially Lyndon Johnson vastly increased the number of American troops fighting in Vietnam.

During the 1968 campaign, President Lyndon Johnson did all he could to help his vice-president win the election. He stopped American planes from bombing cities in Communist North Vietnam. He even said that he had a "secret plan" to end the war, and that a final and just settlement was just around the corner.

When election day came in November, American voters turned away from the Democrats. Although Nixon won the election by only about half a million votes—relatively close for a national election—it would have been a landslide if the governor of Alabama, George Wallace, had not entered the election as an independent candidate. Most political experts agreed that the majority of the nearly ten million votes cast for George Wallace would have gone to Nixon if the Alabama governor had not been in the race.

With his years in the House of Representatives and the Senate, and his particularly active role as vice-president, Richard Nixon was supremely qualified to be president. But America was a nation in serious trouble. President-elect Richard Nixon knew that his job in the White House would be a tough one indeed!

Chapter 6

FROM PRESIDENT TO PRIVATE RESIDENT

On January 20, 1969, the Nixons drove to the White House to have coffee and rolls with the retiring President Lyndon Johnson and his wife, Lady Bird. Then it was on to the Capitol Building, where Richard Nixon was officially sworn in as the thirty-seventh president of the United States. Also in the ceremony was Spiro T. Agnew, the new vice-president.

Hundreds of antiwar demonstrators lined the Washington streets as the Nixons drove back to the White House, their new home for at least the next four years. A few threw rocks and empty cans as the presidential car drove by. It was clear that President Nixon had a great deal of work ahead of him to bring the country back together again.

His work had started weeks earlier, almost immediately after the election. Before he even took office, President-elect Nixon began to choose the people who would be his top assistants. Some of the most important people who help the president are in the cabinet. Each cabinet member is the leader of a large department of the federal government. Some of Nixon's most important choices included William Rogers, secretary of state; Melvin Laird, secretary of defense; and John Mitchell, attorney general. Henry Kissinger became President Nixon's National Security Adviser, because of his knowledge of foreign nations and their problems.

With all his assistants to help him, Nixon knew that he would never have to face great problems alone, although he alone would have to make many final decisions. To help keep track of all the assistants, Nixon asked a young man who had helped in his campaign, Bob Haldeman, to be his chief of staff.

The new president would need these people, and many others, to help solve the serious problems facing the United States. Nixon feared that it might be difficult to work with Congress. For the first time since Zachary Taylor had been president in the 1850s, a new president had come to office with both the Senate and House of Representatives controlled by the opposing party. Among the Democrats in Congress, there was a growing desire to get out of the war in Vietnam regardless of the consequences. Nixon strongly disagreed with this trend.

Despite the urgent business ahead, it had to be exciting for Richard Nixon and his family to move into the historic White House. Ever since John Adams had been president in the 1820s, each new president and his family had lived and worked in the White House. When Theodore Roosevelt was president in the early 1900s, he added the West Wing, a three-story building housing some of the best-known rooms in the White House, including the Oval Office and the Cabinet Room. An East Wing, with offices for the First Lady and the president's staff, was added during World War II. From the Lincoln Sitting Room to Eisenhower's bed, the White House was filled with history and tradition.

Even though he had worked closely with President Eisenhower during the 1950s as his vice-president, the new president had much to learn about the life-style of the nation's top officeholder. The president is surrounded by aides wherever he goes. When he came to office, Nixon discovered that two men were employed full time just to rub the president's back! When the president traveled away from the White House, his bed was flown ahead so that he could sleep in it wherever he might be. The navy kept two large boats ready in case the president felt the need to relax aboard one. Of course, dozens of Secret Service men were employed to protect the president and his family from any dangers. And there would be people to help with the cooking, cleaning, and gardening, and even to help the president get dressed!

There was a reason for this seeming madness. Faced with difficult decisions day and night that could change the lives of millions of people, a president had to concentrate on the business of America, not on personal problems. Nevertheless, President Nixon put a stop to many of these expensive traditions.

In 1969, the most urgent business facing the new president was to find a way to end the Vietnam War without allowing the government of South Vietnam to be defeated by Communists. Under Lyndon Johnson, the United States had fought a tough, but limited, war. Every effort was made not to injure people who were not involved in the fighting, and not to bring other, perhaps unfriendly, nations into the war.

President Nixon decided that these rules made it difficult for the non-Communist forces fighting in South Vietnam to defeat the Communists. In March of 1969, he ordered B-52 airplanes to drop huge bombs on parts of the nation of Cambodia. Those areas of Cambodia were being used as hiding places for Communist soldiers fighting in South Vietnam. A number of people in Congress were angered that he seemed to be making the unpopular war even more widespread. Nixon argued that he was only trying to bring a swift end to the fighting. About a year later, he ordered American troops to invade those same areas of Cambodia to find the Communist troops hiding in the jungle there.

The United States-led invasion of Cambodia touched off huge anti-war protests all across the country, especially on college campuses. Some demonstrators used the same methods they were protesting against when they destroyed a number of college buildings with bombs and fires. Nixon was thinking of these kinds of protesters when he called many of the young demonstrators "bums" in a speech that was widely reported in the news.

A few days after the Cambodian invasion, two young men at Ohio's Kent State University burned down a campus building used by the army. At the same time, many other Kent State students were involved in a more or less peaceful demonstration against the war in Vietnam. For reasons that are hard to understand, soldiers in the Ohio National Guard opened fire on the unarmed students and shot four of them dead. In a tearful interview with radio and television reporters, the father of one of the slain students sobbed, "My child was not a 'bum.'" Nixon was greatly saddened by the tragedy. He wrote personal letters to the families of each of the students who was killed.

From the beginning of his presidency, Nixon was troubled by what are often called "news leaks." Especially concerning the Vietnam War, he was shocked to find discussions with his aides that he thought were private repeated very accurately in newspapers and television newscasts all across the country.

Around April of 1969, he spoke with the director of the Federal Bureau of Investigation, J. Edgar Hoover, about the problem. Hoover said that one solution would be to listen in on, or "tap," the phone conversations of people working for the president. Nixon was surprised to hear Hoover say that every American president since Franklin Roosevelt had tapped phone conversations. Nixon decided to do the same.

Even earlier, President Nixon had decided to place hidden microphones in a number of White House offices to make tape recordings of the conversations he held there. Presidents Roosevelt, Eisenhower, Kennedy, and Johnson had made recordings of at least some of their conversations. Again, Nixon would do the same, but he would record far more conversations than any other president. In a few more years, the famous tape recordings, which would become known as the "White House tapes," would do much to destroy Nixon's presidency.

During his first term in office, however, Nixon kept his tape recordings secret. Few people in the White House realized that their voices were being recorded. Nixon felt that the tapes would make an excellent record of his presidency, and, possibly, would help to find people who were leaking private information, especially about the Vietnam War, to the press.

Four presidents—Eisenhower, Kennedy, Johnson, and Nixon—had worked with the problem of Communists in Vietnam. None had yet been able to solve it, nor would Richard Nixon. Near the end of his presidency, Nixon would finally end the war, but he would not stop the Communists from taking over the country. For this reason, Nixon's decisions about Vietnam were not, in the end, successful ones. But in many other areas of government, his ideas and hard work led to very successful new programs.

Throughout his political life, Nixon had been very distrustful of Communist governments throughout the world. As president, he still had little faith in the honesty and goodwill of Communist leaders, but he also realized the need for America to keep communicating with Communist nations. Despite the major differences between the two systems of government, he knew that the best way to avoid war was for each nation to try to understand the other, regardless of political beliefs.

Since the end of World War II, no American president had visited a Communist nation while in office. Richard Nixon ended that tradition when, in February of 1972, he visited Communist China. There, he would meet Mao Zedong, the elderly Communist leader of the most populous nation on earth.

Chairman Mao, as he was known, lived in the great city of Peking, the capital of China. When Nixon's airplane arrived at Peking airport, it was met by Mao's most important helper, Zhou Enlai. Knowing that American officials in the past had refused to shake hands with Zhou Enlai, Nixon walked up to the old man and shook his hand as soon as he left his plane.

As an automobile carrying Zhou and the American president left the airport and drove toward the center of Peking,

Zhou looked warmly at Nixon. "Your handshake came over the vastest ocean in the world," the Chinese leader said, "twenty-five years of no communication."

Soon after Nixon had settled into the guest house reserved for the American visitors, his aide Henry Kissinger burst into the room. Kissinger reported that Chairman Mao would like to speak with Nixon. Before long, the Chinese chairman and the American president, supposed enemies, were having a merry discussion and making jokes. Both men had written books. Henry Kissinger said that he had assigned one of Mao's books to his students at Harvard.

"These writings of mine aren't anything," Mao remarked.

Richard Nixon replied, "The chairman's writings moved a nation and changed the world."

"I haven't been able to change it," the powerful Chinese leader answered. "I've only been able to change a few places around Peking." For such an important leader, it was a very modest joke to make.

The Americans stayed in China for a week. In the many discussions that took place, it was not possible to end all the differences that existed between the two nations. But it may be that the seeds of a new friendship had been sown. For too long, two giant nations had refused to communicate.

In his final meeting with his Chinese hosts, Nixon summed up his hope for the future. "We have been here a week," he said. "This was the week that changed the world."

Just a few months after his visit to China, Nixon made his second visit to Russia, his first as president. Nikita Khrushchev had died since his last visit, so Nixon met with the new Russian leader, Leonid Brezhnev. As always, relations between Russia and the United States were not good.

At the time of his visit, Russia was building a huge number of nuclear missiles. The United States military, afraid of falling behind in the arms race, was pressing the president to spend billions of dollars to make more American missiles. American military officials were also very distrustful of Russian leaders.

If at all possible, Nixon wanted to avoid a costly missile race. Even though the Russians were extremely angry with the U.S. about the Vietnam War, President Nixon managed to start a number of important agreements with Russia to limit the construction of nuclear missiles by both countries. The agreements were extremely important. Although in the 1980s both the United States and Russia would once again be building many dangerous and costly weapons, Nixon's efforts saved billions of dollars and made the world safer for nearly a decade.

Despite this success, Nixon knew that he was visiting a strange and unfriendly country. The Russians did not even try to hide the fact that they had microphones hidden in the guest rooms the Americans stayed in. Once, one of Nixon's aides told his secretary that he would like to have an apple.

Although no one else had been present, a Russian maid brought in a bowl of apples a few minutes later.

Under the Russian system of government, everyone is supposed to be treated equally. But Nixon couldn't help noticing that some Russians were treated more equally than others. In many of Moscow's streets, a center lane was made available so that members of the Communist party could drive their automobiles past traffic jams. Nevertheless, Nixon left Russia with the hope that the world's two most powerful nations could learn to live together in peace. Nixon himself had gone a long way in making this possible. The first Strategic Arms Limitation Treaty, known as the SALT agreement, was made final on October 3, 1972.

In June of 1972, when Nixon returned from his successful visit to Russia, he knew that he had to begin campaigning to win the presidential election scheduled for November of that year. Knowing better than any other American how tough political campaigns could be, he decided to take a short vacation. He would have to go without his family. His daughters Tricia and Julie were both married now. Pat was on the West Coast campaigning and making other appearances for him.

After visiting Grand Cay, an island in the Bahamas, Nixon and a friend went to Key Biscayne, a small island south of the Florida mainland. While he was there, on Sunday morning June 18, he began reading a copy of the *Miami*

Herald newspaper. On the front page was a small but peculiar story.

Five men, according to the report, had been arrested at the Democratic National Headquarters in Washington's Watergate Hotel. The story suggested that the men had been trying to plant electronic "bugs," or microphones, in the Democratic offices. One of the burglars said that he was once an employee of the Central Intelligence Agency. The others were former Cubans living in Miami.

Nixon didn't think about the story very much. It seemed odd, but he soon forgot about it. He planned to return to the White House that night, but the weather was bad and so he decided to stay on Key Biscayne for another day. Instead of getting ready to return, he made phone calls to his daughters and to some of his aides.

As he was returning to Washington the following day, he learned some disturbing news from his chief of staff, Bob Haldeman. One of the men arrested for breaking into the Democratic headquarters at the Watergate Hotel was working for the Committee to Re-Elect President Nixon. The next day, June 20, the *Washington Post* carried a story that a notebook held by one of the burglars included the name E. Howard Hunt. Hunt had worked for one of Richard Nixon's aides, Charles Colson.

Suddenly, it looked as if the White House, and possibly even the president himself, might in some way be connected with an illegal break-in at the Democratic headquarters. With the election approaching, Nixon now realized that he might have a real problem on his hands.

That same afternoon and evening, Nixon held two meetings with Bob Haldeman. More than a year later, these meetings would become famous. When the Watergate crisis reached its height, many investigators were trying to find out just how much the president knew about the break-in shortly after it happened. They wanted to know what Haldeman told Nixon during these two meetings on June 20. In order to find out, they went through a long legal battle to get the tapes that had recorded so many conversations in the White House. But the tape of the Nixon-Haldeman meeting had a strange eighteen-minute gap that no one, including the president, could explain. Some experts said the tape had been erased.

Of course, this all happened much later. At the time, few people knew that the tapes existed. In his autobiography, Nixon explained the things he could remember from his meetings with Haldeman. Haldeman had some information, Nixon wrote, but did not know all the details about the break-in.

At some point around this time, Nixon began to realize that the Democrats might use the Watergate affair to try to defeat him in the 1972 presidential election. Nixon felt that he had done a good job as president, and that he deserved to be reelected. He could not let the Watergate affair ruin his chances. Therefore, he would do everything he could to show that he had not been involved in Watergate.

As more and more details of the Watergate break-in were discovered, it seemed that Nixon was trying to cover something up. Eventually, he would be accused of "obstructing justice," that is, trying to hide facts from people investigating a crime. If he had admitted everything he knew from the beginning, he would certainly have escaped the shame of his final year in office. And, contrary to what he believed at the time, it seems unlikely that the Watergate break-in could have seriously hurt his chances for reelection, even if he told the American people the full truth.

There can be little doubt that America was much better off after four years of the Nixon presidency than it had been before he took office. Although he had not been able to end the war in Vietnam, far fewer Americans were fighting and dying there than when he took office. Only one sixth as many Americans were drafted into the military in 1972 as in 1968, when Nixon was about to take office. Antiwar protests were, at last, slowing down.

During the earliest years of the Nixon presidency, the American economy had serious problems. Inflation was at dangerously high levels. Some people were losing their jobs. In an unusual move for a Republican president, Nixon made a startling announcement on August 15, 1971. The prices of all goods and services, as well as the wages of most Americans, would be frozen for a period of ninety days. During this period, stores could not raise the prices of any of the items they sold, and workers could not ask for higher salaries. After ninety days, he asked all Americans to follow his ideas for changing prices and salaries very carefully.

The unusual move, which sounded much like the economic controls used by Communist governments, worked. Inflation was cut by more than half. Unemployment, which had been rising, went down. The stock market rose. As the wage and price controls were gradually removed (they are almost never removed in Communist nations), the effective income of Americans increased for the first time in more than seven years. Income taxes for poor and average Americans were greatly cut, too.

In 1968, when Nixon won his first presidential election, nearly half of the money spent by the federal government went to defense and war. Only about one third was spent on things such as education, social welfare, and health care. By 1972 and 1973, these proportions had been reversed. Nixon had also tried to begin an important new welfare program that would surely have improved life for the nation's poor, but the Democratic Congress refused to allow it to become a law.

The elections of 1972 showed that most Americans believed Nixon had done a good job as president. Although the

Watergate break-in and the investigation that followed it were in the news throughout the 1972 campaign, few Americans were greatly worried.

At the Republican National Convention in Miami, Florida, Nixon won his party's nomination to run for a second term as president by a vote of 1,347 to 1. At that convention, a slogan that has been used many times since was heard for the first time. "Four more years! Four more years!" It was a chant calling for Nixon to win the November election and go back to the White House for another four-year term. Although he and his vice-presidential running mate, Spiro T. Agnew, would win the election, neither man would be able to stay in office for the full four years.

At their convention, the Democrats nominated Senator George McGovern as their candidate for president. His vice-presidential running mate was another senator, Thomas Eagleton. From the beginning, the Democratic candidates seemed doomed to fail. On July 25, McGovern and Eagleton held a meeting with reporters to admit that Eagleton had been a patient in a mental hospital three times, and that he still took medication to control a mental problem known as depression.

For a few days, McGovern continued to support his vice-presidential running mate. But soon enough, Eagleton was forced to give up his nomination. The millions of Americans who saw Thomas Eagleton rudely questioned by reporters had to admit that he seemed anything but mentally ill. But despite Eagleton's brave attempt to hold on to his nomination, by the first days of August McGovern was searching frantically for a new running mate. Edward Kennedy, the last living brother of President John Kennedy, refused McGovern's offer. So did at least five other Democratic politicians. Finally, a brother-in-law of Edward Kennedy, Sargent Shriver, accepted McGovern's offer.

After a terrible beginning, the Democratic campaign never seemed to get rolling. During the campaign, Republicans were in the news almost daily, for reasons that were both good and not so good. The Democrats were hardly noticed at all.

On September 15, 1972, the first formal charges, or indictments, were made against seven people involved in the break-in of the Watergate Hotel. More than 300 agents from the Federal Bureau of Investigation had interviewed more than 1,500 people to examine every detail of the break-in. Remarkably, the FBI found that no one at the White House was involved. In the months to come, it would be discovered that many people at the White House were involved in allowing the break-in to happen and then in covering it up.

October started out as a good month for President Nixon. On October 3 an important Russian official, Andrei Gromyko, arrived in Washington to sign the SALT agreement Nixon had worked so hard to develop on his last visit to

Russia. The SALT agreement would limit the number of nuclear weapons to be built by both the United States and Russia.

Later in October, however, two stories were printed in the *Washington Post* that eventually would be very damaging to Nixon. The first story said that a young lawyer named Donald Segretti had been hired by a Nixon aide to play "dirty tricks" on Democratic candidates and their families. The tricks involved sending out phony letters making Democrats sound immoral or stupid, and even stealing confidential Democratic papers.

The *Washington Post* ran the second, even more damaging, story on October 25. Two young reporters named Bob Woodward and Carl Bernstein wrote that Bob Haldeman, Nixon's chief of staff, had a secret supply of money to pay for spying and dirty tricks on the Democrats. The story suggested, but did not clearly state, that some of the money may have been used to finance the break-in at the Watergate Hotel. If the suggestion proved true, it would show that money for the illegal break-in had come directly from the Nixon White House.

The *Washington Post* stories indicated that there might be serious problems in the White House. But the reports had little effect on the 1972 vote for president. On election day, Nixon defeated George McGovern in the largest Republican landslide in history. Only the District of Columbia and the state of Massachusetts voted for McGovern. The other forty-nine states were solidly for Nixon. The team of Richard Nixon and Spiro Agnew had won, and won big. But there would be few victories left for either man.

In the months following the election, the Watergate stories seemed to die down a bit. Only a few newspapers such as the *New York Times* and especially the *Washington Post* seemed interested in continuing the investigation. Nixon believed that he would be able to survive the crisis.

Meanwhile Nixon and many of the people under him worked desperately to end the Vietnam War without handing South Vietnam to the Communists. Americans had fought this war longer than any other conflict in the nation's history. Few wanted it to last much longer.

Nixon knew he had to end the war quickly. Almost immediately after New Year's Day, 1973, committees in both the House of Representatives and the Senate voted to cut off all the money needed to continue the fighting. Soon, the full Congress would vote on the matter, and more and more people in Congress wanted the war to end immediately.

In a last-ditch effort to defeat the Communists, Nixon had ordered powerful bombing raids on Communist positions all over Vietnam. But the Communists still refused to give up. On January 15, he ordered the bombing stopped, partly because huge demonstrations against the war began again in the United States.

For months, Henry Kissinger had tried to talk with the Communist government of North Vietnam and the non-Communist government in South Vietnam to find a way to end the war. For a brief time, it looked as if he might make a settlement in which South Vietnam would be governed by both Communists and non-Communists. But in the end, the South Vietnamese government in Saigon refused to go along with the agreement made by the United States and North Vietnam. At the end of January, the few remaining American soldiers in South Vietnam all stopped fighting.

Soon, the last Americans in Saigon had to be carried away by helicopter to avoid being slaughtered by the Communist soldiers entering the city. South Vietnam and North Vietnam were united as a single Communist nation. For the first time in its history, America had clearly lost a war.

The war in Vietnam was lost, but Nixon's battle to save his presidency was just beginning. In March of 1973, a meeting of Democratic senators was held. During the conference, the senators voted to begin an investigation of the 1972 Republican campaign and the Watergate break-in. Selected to head the investigation was Senator Sam Ervin of North Carolina.

Before long, Nixon's top aides in the White House knew that they would be called before the Senate committee to answer pointed questions under oath. Suddenly, each man felt he had things to tell his boss. On March 20, Bob Haldeman told the president about a fund of $350,000 taken from Nixon campaign contributions and brought to the White House for reasons that were not entirely clear.

The very next day, the official lawyer for the White House, John Dean III, opened a discussion with the president by saying, "We have a cancer—within—close to the presidency, that's growing. It's growing daily." In his shocking speech, Dean suggested that Nixon's attorney-general, John Mitchell, knew about the burglary before it took place. Mitchell was the man with the direct responsibility of seeing that the laws of the nation were obeyed. This man had possibly permitted a burglary to take place.

Dean also said that one of the men involved in the Watergate break-in, E. Howard Hunt, was threatening to tell everything he knew unless he got $122,000.

Two days after Nixon's meeting with John Dean, Washington Judge John Sirica passed sentence on the Watergate burglars. Each of the men was given a sentence of between thirty-five and forty years in jail. Many murderers got away with less. The stiff sentences were designed to make the burglars talk, but there was little need for it. At the Senate committee hearings investigating the whole affair, almost everyone was talking.

The best talker of all at the nationally televised hearings was John Dean. In great detail, Dean explained how many people in the White House, including himself and President

Nixon, had probably broken the law. Some of the committee members were outraged by the things Dean said. Some thought he might even be lying. Nevertheless many of the committee members felt there was enough truth in what Dean said to wonder seriously whether the president should stay in office.

With the Senate investigation underway, many of Nixon's top aides were forced to quit. Two of the men closest to the president, Bob Haldeman and John Ehrlichman, were forced to resign on April 30. Both men tried to save their jobs by threatening to reveal damaging information, but it was no use. John Dean was fired the same day.

By the dozens, more people were called before the Senate Watergate committee. Some still worked at the White House. Many had been fired or had quit. But few would confirm the things that John Dean had said. Some, especially John Ehrlichman and Bob Haldeman, refused to answer many of the questions they were asked because, they said, it would harm "national security." Many members of the committee did not know what to believe.

President Nixon, realizing that he was in serious trouble, refused to cooperate with the investigation committee's requests for information. The investigation seemed to be at a standstill. But on July 16, 1973, members of the committee made an astounding discovery. For the first time, they learned from a former aide to Bob Haldeman that tapes existed of all the major discussions in the White House. Americans all over the country learned the astounding news that same day. Now it would be possible to find out how much Nixon had known about Watergate—merely by listening to the tapes!

There was, however, one problem. President Nixon had no intention of letting go of the damaging tapes. Considering the trouble they were about to cause him, it is hard to understand why he kept them for so long. Nixon later wrote that he was shocked to hear that the Senate committee knew about the tapes. "As impossible as it may seem now," he wrote, "I had believed that the existence of the White House taping system would never be revealed."

The battle for the White House tapes created a major crisis in the United States government. Leaders in two branches of the federal government—the executive (President Nixon) and the legislative (the Senate)—were at odds. Even the Constitution gave no clear advice about how to settle such an argument. It would have to be settled in the courts.

On August 29, Washington Judge Sirica ordered Nixon to give up the tapes. Lawyers for the president asked a higher court to change the decision. That court also ruled against the president, but before it reached its decision on October 12, 1973, there was yet another shocking blow to Nixon's presidency.

With very little notice to anyone outside of government,

Vice-President Spiro T. Agnew announced on October 10, 1973, that he was quitting. Criminal charges had been made against him and he had no defense. Some years earlier, when he was governor of Maryland, Agnew had taken bribes from people doing business with his state government. He had also failed to pay income taxes on these bribes.

With all the other problems facing him, Nixon now had to find a new vice-president. The person he chose would have to be approved by Congress before taking office. President Nixon had a number of choices for a new vice-president. One of them was the governor of California and a future president, Ronald Reagan. But the Democrats in Congress did not want him to be vice-president. They knew that in a matter of months the new vice-president might replace Richard Nixon. They wanted someone a Democrat could beat in the 1976 elections—someone who would be capable of leading the country, but would probably not be able to win an election for president.

Finally Nixon nominated Congressman Gerald R. Ford on October 12, 1973. About two months later, on December 6, Congress approved the nomination. Gerald Ford was the new vice-president of the United States.

In the meantime, President Nixon's problems grew worse and worse. On October 20, Nixon tried to fire a special prosecutor investigating the Watergate affair. When he asked the attorney general, Elliot Richardson, to do the firing,

Richardson quit instead. Deputy Attorney General William Ruckelshaus also refused and was fired. The sad event became known as the "Saturday-Night Massacre."

Within a few days, dozens of Congressmen were calling for Nixon's impeachment. Under the United States Constitution a president may be impeached, or put on trial, by the House of Representatives and the Senate. Members of the House must make charges against the president. When the charges are agreed upon, certain members of the House are selected to appear before the Senate to act as managers for the trial. After the trial, the senators take a vote. If two thirds of them vote to convict the president of wrongdoing, he or she can be removed from office.

Five days after the Saturday-Night Massacre, President Nixon put America's armed forces on alert. A military alert is a warning that American troops may have to go to war. Many people worried about the president. Perhaps the pressure of impeachment was just too much for him.

But the president had good reason for his actions. He called for a military alert because the country of Israel had been attacked by a number of its neighboring nations. Under his guidance, American airplanes brought needed supplies to Israel and may have saved it from destruction. Despite his incredible problems, President Nixon showed great decisiveness when he helped Israel defend itself.

But it was becoming almost impossible for the president

to defend himself. On March 1, 1974, many of the men who were once top Nixon aides, including Haldeman, Ehrlichman, and Mitchell, were officially charged with serious crimes. All would eventually go to jail.

By April, a poll showed that the majority of Americans, for the first time, thought Nixon should be impeached. Congress was still demanding the White House tapes, and Nixon was still refusing. In a last-ditch effort to soothe an angry Congress, Nixon released typed versions of some of the taped conversations. But the typed pages were not satisfactory as far as the Congress was concerned. Most of its members still wanted the tapes.

In June, Nixon made a final trip as president to the countries of the Middle East and to Russia. In the Middle East, he visited some of the nations that Henry Kissinger had recently talked into signing a peace treaty. In Russia, he worked on another treaty himself.

When he returned, he could see that his presidency was all but lost. Most members of the House of Representatives, even Republicans, were ready to vote for impeachment. Soon, the United States Supreme Court ruled that he would have to give up the White House tapes. His long battle to keep them private had been lost. There was no higher court to turn to. By the end of July, members of the House of Representatives were already writing formal charges of impeachment.

By the first days of August, the White House had become a strange place indeed. Most of his old friends and aides were gone. Many were facing trial and jail. Only a few of the important people from his first term, such as Henry Kissinger, remained. In the final days, his family came together to be by his side. Julie and her husband were there, as were Tricia and her husband. Pat did what she could to cheer her husband. All said how much they loved him. The children, who were hardly children any longer, encouraged their father not to give up the fight. But all must have known the end was near.

On August 8, 1974, the Nixons' last full day in the White House, the president worked on his final speech to be made as president, while Gerald Ford met with the members of the cabinet to keep the business of governing America moving. At 7:30 in the evening, Nixon met with leaders of Congress to tell them officially that he was resigning. An hour and a half later, he went on national television to give a short resignation speech. He announced that he would be resigning the presidency at noon the following day.

Then, he knew, a helicopter would take him and Pat to the airport, where he would board a plane bound for California. He may not have known that, a month later, Gerald Ford would use the power of the presidency to pardon him for all wrongdoing he may have committed as president. If the pardon had not been made, Nixon would certainly have faced years of trials and lawsuits.

When his speech was completed, the bright television lights blinked off. As he walked out of the Oval Office, he found his old friend Henry Kissinger waiting for him in the hallway.

"Mr. President," Kissinger said in his deep German accent, "after most of your major speeches in this office we have walked together back to your house. I would be honored to walk with you again tonight."

On the way back to the White House living quarters, Kissinger remarked that history would judge Nixon as one of the great presidents. The president turned to him and said, "That depends, Henry, on who writes the history."

It may also depend on who reads it.

Richard Milhous Nixon 1913-

1913 Richard Milhous Nixon is born in Yorba Linda, California. U.S. passes sixteenth amendment, instituting income taxes, and seventeenth amendment, providing for election of senators by popular vote.

1914 Archduke Francis Ferdinand is assassinated in Sarajevo, Yugoslavia; World War I begins.

1915 Germans sink the *Lusitania* and U.S. merchant ships and blockade Britain with submarines.

1916 Woodrow Wilson is reelected president.

1917 U.S. declares war on Germany and enters World War I.

1918 World War I ends.

1919 U.S. passes eighteenth amendment, prohibiting sale of alcoholic beverages. First League of Nations meeting is held in Paris.

1920 Warren G. Harding is elected president. U.S. passes nineteenth amendment, giving women the right to vote.

1922 Union of Soviet Socialist Republics (commonly called Russia) is formed.

1923 President Warren G. Harding dies; Calvin Coolidge becomes president. Nazi party leader Adolf Hitler is imprisoned for unsuccessful coup attempt, the "Beer Hall Putsch."

1924 Calvin Coolidge is elected president. J. Edgar Hoover heads the Bureau of Investigation (later the Federal Bureau of Investigation). U.S. severely restricts immigration.

1925 Schoolteacher John Scopes is convicted for teaching evolution theory, but is later acquitted.

1927 Charles A. Lindbergh makes first solo transatlantic airplane flight.

1928 Herbert Hoover is elected president.

1929 U.S. stock market crashes; worldwide economic crisis follows.

1930 More than 1,300 U.S. banks close due to stock market crash. Hitler's Nazi party gains a majority in German elections.

1932 Franklin D. Roosevelt wins landslide presidential victory.

1933 U.S. passes twenty-first amendment, repealing Prohibition.

1934 Nixon graduates from Whittier College in California.

1936 Franklin D. Roosevelt is reelected president.

1937 Nixon receives law degree from Duke University Law School.

1939 World War II begins.

1940 Roosevelt is reelected president for a third term. Nixon marries Thelma (Pat) Ryan.

1941 U.S. Office of Price Administration is established.

1942 Nixon joins the navy.

1945 Franklin D. Roosevelt dies; vice-president Harry Truman becomes president. U.S. drops first atomic bombs on Hiroshima and Nagasaki, Japan; Hitler commits suicide; Mussolini is killed; Germany and Japan surrender to Allies; World War II ends.

1946 Nixon is elected to the House of Representatives. Winston Churchill gives "Iron Curtain" speech.

1947 U.S. Secretary of State George Marshall proposes the European Recovery Program, also called the Marshall Plan.

1948 Harry Truman is elected president. Congress approves $17 billion for European aid under the

Marshall Plan. Whittaker Chambers accuses Alger Hiss of being a spy.

1949 Eleven Communists in the U.S. are convicted of conspiracy to overthrow the government.

1950 Nixon is elected to U.S. Senate. Senator Joseph McCarthy charges that Communists have infiltrated the U.S. State Department. Former U.S. State Department official Alger Hiss is convicted of perjury. Korean War begins; Douglas MacArthur commands UN forces in Korea. U.S. agrees to send arms and troops to Vietnam.

1951 Congress passes twenty-second amendment, setting two terms (eight years) as the maximum service for president. Color television is introduced in the U.S.

1952 Dwight D. Eisenhower is elected president, with Nixon as vice-president. Korean Armistice ends war. King George VI of England dies; his daughter becomes Queen Elizabeth II.

1953 Joseph Stalin dies; Nikita Khrushchev becomes head of Soviet Communist party Central Committee.

1954 Senator Joseph McCarthy accuses U.S. army of Communist infiltration. Communists in Vietnam take Dien Bien Phu and occupy Hanoi.

1955 President Eisenhower suffers a heart attack. U.S. begins sending aid to Vietnam. Dictator Peron of Argentina is overthrown.

1956 Eisenhower is reelected president. Hungarians revolt against Russian occupation; Soviet troops invade Hungary. Israeli army invades Sinai Peninsula. Pakistan declares itself an Islamic nation. Gamal Abdul Nassar becomes president of Egypt.

1957 Andrei Gromyko becomes Soviet foreign minister. Soviets launch first man-made satellites, *Sputnik I* and *II*. European Common Market is established.

1958 Vice-president Nixon makes goodwill tour of South America. U.S. launches its first satellite. Alaska becomes forty-ninth state. Khrushchev becomes chairman of Soviet Council of Ministers. Charles de Gaulle becomes president of France.

1959 Hawaii becomes fiftieth state. Fidel Castro overthrows Cuban dictator Batista and becomes president.

1960 Richard Nixon and John F. Kennedy hold first television debates between presidential candidates; Kennedy defeats Nixon in presidential election. Lenoid Brezhnev becomes president of U.S.S.R.

1961 Nixon begins law practice in Los Angeles. U.S. breaks diplomatic ties with Cuba.

1962 Nixon loses California gubernatorial election to Pat Brown. U.S. establishes military advisors in South Vietnam.

1963 President Kennedy is assassinated in Dallas; Lyndon B. Johnson becomes president. Race riots and demonstrations in Birmingham, Alabama, lead to the arrest of Martin Luther King, Jr.

1964 Lyndon B. Johnson is elected president. Vietnamese war escalates. Khrushchev loses some power in U.S.S.R.: Alexei Kosygin becomes prime minister and Brezhnev becomes Communist party secretary.

1965 Race riots leave thirty-five dead in Watts district of Los Angeles; racial violence breaks out in Selma, Alabama. Russia supplies arms to North Vietnam; North Vietnamese aircraft destroy U.S. jets; anti-war demonstrations sweep U.S.

1966 President Johnson tours the Far East.

1967 U.S. bombs Hanoi, North Vietnam. Arab nations and Israel engage in Six-Day War. 50,000 demonstrate against the Vietnam War at the Lincoln Memorial in Washington, D.C.

1968 Nixon is elected president. Martin Luther King, Jr., is shot in Memphis. Senator Robert Kennedy is shot in Los Angeles. *Apollo 8* is the first spacecraft to orbit the moon. Russia invades and occupies Czechoslovakia.

1969 Neil Armstrong is the first man to walk on the moon.

1970 Five students at Kent State University in Ohio are shot by National Guard during anti-war demonstrations.

1971 Nixon institutes a wage-price freeze. People's Republic of China is admitted to United Nations.

1972 Nixon is reelected president; he reinstates diplomatic relations with China, and is the first president to visit China and Moscow. Burglars break into Democratic party headquarters in Washington's Watergate Hotel.

1973 Watergate break-in comes to light; Nixon aides Ehrlichman and Haldeman resign; House Judiciary Committee begins impeachment hearings. Vice-president Agnew resigns in income tax scandal; Gerald Ford becomes vice-president. Cease-fire is declared in Vietnam. Middle East unrest causes oil prices to double, creating energy crisis.

1974 Nixon resigns presidency; Gerald Ford becomes president and pardons Nixon. Arabs lift oil embargo to the West.

1975 Vietnamese War ends with South Vietnam's surrender to North Vietnam.

1976 Jimmy Carter is elected president. North and South Vietnam are united as Socialist Republic of Vietnam, with Hanoi as capital. U.S. and U.S.S.R. sign a nuclear arms limitation treaty. Reporters Bob Woodward and Carl Bernstein publish *The Final Days*, about Nixon's last days in office.

1977 Nixon appears in nationally televised interviews with British commentator David Frost, and makes his first public comments on Watergate since his resignation. Supreme Court upholds 1974 ruling that the U.S. government has the rights to Nixon's presidential papers and tapes.

1978 Nixon publishes *RN: The Memoirs of Richard Nixon*.

1980 Ronald Reagan is elected president. Nixon moves to New York City; he publishes *The Real War*, about U.S. foreign policy.

1982 Nixon visits China to commemorate tenth anniversary of reinstatement of U.S.-Chinese relations. Nixon publishes *Leaders*, about statesmen he has known. Supreme Court rules that a president cannot be sued for actions done while in office.

INDEX- *Page numbers in boldface type indicate illustrations.*

ABOUT THE AUTHOR

Jim Hargrove has worked as a writer and editor for more than 10 years. After serving as an editorial director for three Chicago area publishers, he began a career as an independent writer, preparing a series of books for children. He has contributed to works by nearly 20 different publishers. His Childrens Press titles are *Mark Twain: The Story of Samuel Clemens* and *Microcomputers at Work*. With his wife and 13-year-old daughter, he lives in a small Illinois town near the Wisconsin border.